Our Economic System

America's Best for Student Success

Triumph Learning®

Our Economic System
296
ISBN-10: 0-87694-390-3
ISBN-13: 978-0-87694-390-8

Triumph Learning® 136 Madison Avenue, 7th Floor, New York, NY 10016
Kevin McAliley, President and Chief Executive Officer

Printed in the United States of America.

10 9 8

TABLE OF CONTENTS

Introduction 5

Chapter 1   ECONOMICS IN OUR WORLD 6

Chapter 2   FOUR ECONOMIC QUESTIONS 14

Chapter 3   ECONOMIC SYSTEMS 20

Chapter 4   THE U.S. ECONOMIC SYSTEM 30

Chapter 5   DEMAND IN A MARKET ECONOMY 38

Chapter 6   SUPPLY IN A MARKET ECONOMY 48

Chapter 7   PRICES IN A MARKET ECONOMY 56

Chapter 8   EARNING MONEY IN A MARKET ECONOMY 62

Chapter 9   MONEY: WHO NEEDS IT? 70

Chapter 10   BUSINESS AND INVESTMENT IN A MARKET ECONOMY 78

Chapter 11   COMPETITION 90

Chapter 12   INCOME IN THE UNITED STATES 100

Chapter 13   LABOR IN A MARKET ECONOMY 108

Chapter 14   WHO DOESN'T HAVE A JOB? 116

Chapter 15   WORKER ORGANIZATIONS 124

Chapter 16   PAYING TAXES 136

Chapter 17   USING YOUR MONEY 141

Chapter 18   FINANCIAL INSTITUTIONS 150

INTRODUCTION

Dear Student:

Economics is an important part of your life. In fact, economics influences your life in so many ways it's impossible to count them.

Economics affects what job you do. It affects how much you earn. It affects how you decide to use your money. It affects what you can buy with that money. It affects where and how you live. It affects how goods and services come to you.

There is probably nothing in your daily life that economics doesn't influence in some way!

Yet many students often think of economics as a hard subject to study. It doesn't have to be hard. In this text, I've tried to explain the basic topics and ideas in economics as clearly and simply as possible. In addition, I've included illustrations and charts all through the book. They will help you see—and understand—some of the things that the book is talking about.

I hope you enjoy using this text.

Clairece Feagin
Gainesville, Florida

CHAPTER 1

ECONOMICS IN OUR WORLD

Linda's Thursday

Linda Botero is the young assistant manager of a record store. Let's take a look at a few of the things she did on Thursday last week.

Linda ate three meals, of course. At work she sold audio tapes and CDs to the store's customers. She also ordered tapes and CDs to replace the ones she sold, and she took some of the store's cash to the bank. At lunch time, Linda took her car to a gas station for a tune-up, had her tank filled with gas, and made an appointment to have her hair done on Saturday. After work she picked up some money from a cash machine and went grocery shopping. When Linda got back to her house she paid a few bills and spent the rest of the evening watching TV with a friend.

Every one of these activities involved economics.

What Is Economics?

Economics is about producing and consuming goods and services. It is also about selling and buying these goods and services.

❖ **Goods** = Products; things you can see and touch and use

Here are just a few of the goods that Linda was involved with: food, audio tapes, CDs, cars, gas stations, gasoline, cash machines, houses, and TV sets.

❖ **Services** = Things people do for someone else

Here are some of the services that Linda performed or received: selling tapes and CDs, handling money at a bank, repairing cars, pumping gas, and ringing up groceries at a grocery counter. Clerks, teachers, gas-station attendants, doctors, truck drivers, musicians, and hairdressers are just a few of the people who provide services.

Economics is a part of almost everything that Linda did. It is a part of almost everything you do, too.

Economics influences where you live, what you eat, the clothes you wear, the way you earn money, the kind of transportation you use, even how you spend your time. All these things and many more are shaped by economics.

Figure 1-1 *Examples of Goods and Services*

Making Economic Choices

Economics is also about choices.

A basic question of economics that individuals and groups must answer every day is:

"How will we use our scarce resources to satisfy our needs and wants?"

What are needs? What are wants? What is the difference between the two? What are resources? And what is meant by scarcity?

Physical Needs

Needs, or **physical needs**, are things that are necessary for life.

All people have certain basic physical needs. People need air, water, food, clothing, and shelter. These things are necessary for life.

Some of people's needs—air, for example—are free, although because of pollution, in many places clean air will be available again only at a very high cost. Other needs—such as food, clothing, and shelter—are not free.

The basic needs for food, clothing, and shelter are not exactly the same for all people. For example, people need different kinds of food depending on such things as their age and how active they are. In addition, people in different parts of the world need different kinds of clothing and shelter. In fact, for different groups of people there is a wide variety in the exact definition of basic physical needs.

Figure 1–2 Examples of Needs and Wants

Nevertheless, all people must have some kind of food, clothing, and shelter. These are all considered needs. In order to live, all people's physical needs must be satisfied.

Collective Needs

People living in groups also have **collective needs.** For example, people living in towns or cities need water and sewer systems. They also need fire and police protection.

These collective needs are not necessary for life in quite the same way that air and food are. However, without a safe water supply, a sanitary sewage disposal system, and reliable fire and police protection, the group's health and safety are in danger.

Satisfying these collective needs improves people's quality of life. People can also be more productive members of society when their health and safety needs are met.

Wants

People want many things that are not necessary for life. They want things that will make them happy. They want things that will give them greater comfort of mind and body. These wants are called **psychological wants.**

Of course, not all people want the same things. There is a lot more variety in people's psychological wants than in people's physical needs.

- What people want depends on *when* they live.

Stores in the United States today are full of a wide variety of products that didn't exist when you were born. Every year new products appear. Many of today's products, such as low-cost hand calculators, microwave ovens, personal computers, and home video games did not exist in the 1970s.

Your grandparents and parents lived without many products that almost everyone today wants.

What people want changes as they see new products. And as new products are produced, even more new wants are created. People's wants seem to grow and grow.

- What people want also depends on *where* they live.

Many products that Americans use every day have never been seen or heard of in some other countries. And people in other countries want and use things that most Americans have never heard of.

What Is the Difference Between Needs and Wants?

The line between needs and wants is not always clear. You need food. But do you really need a particular brand of fast-food hamburger? You need clothes. But do you really need designer jeans?

And wants can sometimes become needs. A car is not necessary for life. But a car may be necessary for some people to get to their jobs.

Resources

Resources are what people use to make the things that satisfy their needs and wants. The three basic kinds of resources are:

> - *Natural resources = Things found in nature*
> - *People-made resources = Things made by people and used to make more*
> - *Human resources, or labor*

Natural resources include air, water, land, plants, animals, minerals, and other raw materials.

People-made resources include tools, factories, machinery, and even computers. People-made resources are also called **capital resources** or **capital goods**.

Human resources include the work that people can do, their energy, their ideas, their training, and their skills.

Most products use all of these kinds of resources. For example, a wooden chair began as a tree (natural resource). The tree was cut and milled into lumber by people (human resource) using machinery (people-made resource). Still other workers using different tools crafted the lumber into a chair.

Labor: The Most Important Resource

Human labor is the most important of all resources. Natural resources are important, but natural resources alone cannot produce the products and services that people want to buy. Human labor and skills are necessary. This important point was made by Adam Smith, the father of modern economics.

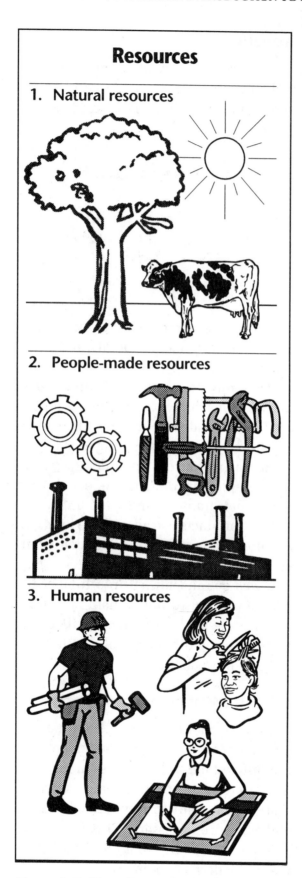

Figure 1–3 Three Types of Resources

Before Smith, economists used to describe a country's wealth in terms of what it possessed—fertile land, minerals, gold, and silver. Then, in 1776, the same year that the U.S. Declaration of Independence was written, Smith published his book *The Wealth of Nations.* Smith wrote that the true wealth of a nation is measured by what the nation *produces,* not what it *possesses.*

Smith showed that what a nation produces, called its **output,** depends mostly on the skills of its workers. In other words, *a nation's wealth is created by the sum total of the labor of its people.*

Smith pointed out that a nation's output is used to satisfy the nation's wants and needs in two ways. Some things are used directly by the nation's people. Other things can be sold to buy goods from other countries.

Satisfying Needs and Wants

Physical needs cannot be permanently satisfied. For example, a few hours after you eat, you are hungry again. Clothing wears out. Shelter also wears out or needs to be repaired.

Psychological wants are usually not permanently satisfied, either. The satisfaction of one want often creates other wants. For example, when frozen foods became available, people wanted bigger and better home refrigerators and freezers.

Cars are another example. Cars may have led to more new wants and brought more changes in our way of life than any other new product. Because of cars, we now have many thousands of miles of streets and highways. Because of cars, large parking areas have been built. Cars have also brought repair shops, car insurance companies, drive-in businesses, travel vacations, and large regional shopping areas.

No matter how many new and wonderful things are produced, society always seems to want more. Consumers—the people who buy products—want more to buy. Businesses—the people who make and sell products—want to make more things to sell. There seems to be no end to society's wants.

Yet the endless needs and wants are what drives economics. If everybody's needs and wants were permanently satisfied, there would be no economics at all.

Progress and Its Side Effects

Improved satisfaction of a society's wants is usually thought of as progress. But progress always has side effects. Not all of the side effects are good.

For example, motor vehicles are an example of progress. Cars make it possible for people to travel from place to place quickly. People use cars to get to work, to shop, and to add pleasure and variety to their lives. Trucks transport goods. Tractors, bulldozers, and other motorized vehicles do much of the nation's work.

But plants that manufacture motor vehicles cause serious air and water pollution. Cars and trucks produce vast amounts of poisonous exhaust fumes. These fumes create serious air pollution and health problems. Fuel for cars uses up large amounts of the world's natural resources. And piles of old cars in junk yards across the country are a major waste disposal problem. These problems are some of the side effects of progress.

Think About It

1. In your notebook, begin making a list of things in your daily life that are shaped by economics. With every chapter you read, you will probably think of something else. At the end of this course, compare your list with those of your classmates.
2. What are physical needs? Name one example.
3. What are collective needs? Name one example.
4. What are psychological wants? Name one example.
5. Name three basic kinds of resources. Give an example of each.

Scarcity

One of the most important concepts in economics is the concept of scarcity. Scarcity exists when there is a gap between needs/wants on the one hand and available resources, goods, or services on the other.

1. **In order for something to be scarce, people must first want it.**

This relationship can be shown using the equals symbol (=) and the greater-than symbol (>).

Scarcity = Wants > Available resources/goods/services

This means that scarcity exists when needs or wants are greater than available resources, goods, or services.

A clothing factory makes 100 shirts of a new design. Are these shirts scarce?

> Yes ___ No ___ Can't tell ___
> *(Answer: Can't tell)*

If more than 100 people want to buy the shirts, the shirts are scarce.

If no one wants to buy a shirt, the shirts are not scarce. Even if the company made only one shirt, it would not be scarce if no one wanted it.

2. In order for something to be scarce, some people who want it must be unable to buy it.

If some people who want shirts don't have enough money to buy shirts, the shirts are scarce for them.

If there are enough shirts for everyone who wants one, and if everyone who wants a shirt has enough money to buy it, then the shirts are not scarce.

3. What is scarce is different at different times and in different places.

A popular rap group makes a CD. Many people want it. Millions of copies sell at a high price. Is the record scarce?

> Yes ___ No ___ Can't tell ___
> *(Answer: Yes)*

Ten years later, people have forgotten about this group. In fact, hardly anyone even remembers the group's name. There are still a few hundred copies of the CD left, but no one wants to buy them. Is the record scarce?

> Yes ___ No ___ Can't tell ___
> *(Answer: No)*

4. Scarcity also involves choosing among a variety of uses for a particular resource.

Almost every resource has more than one possible use.

Consider the many uses of one big pine tree. If the tree is cut down, Planet Earth is minus one pine tree that will never be again. It will give no more shade. It will grow no larger. But unless it is cut down, it is not a resource.

As a resource, the tree can be used for lumber to make buildings or furniture. But no matter how large the tree is, it can make only a limited number of items. Deciding what will be done with the tree is an economic choice.

If we allowed the tree to grow for several more years, it might produce more lumber. Or it might be attacked by insects and become useless as lumber. Deciding when to cut the tree is also an economic choice.

Economic choices such as these are also called **tradeoffs.**

Think About It

1. Make a list of five things that are scarce for you.
2. Explain why each item on your list is scarce for you.
3. Show your list to an adult who is at least 20 years older than you. Are the items that are scarce for you also scarce for this adult? Why or why not?
4. What is meant by *tradeoffs?*

End of Chapter Quiz

Answer True (T) or False (F):

____ 1. Economics is only important to business people and bankers.

____ 2. In economics, *goods* means things you can see and touch and use.

____ 3. In order to live, people's physical *needs* must be satisfied.

____ 4. If you want a stereo because your friend has one, that is called a *collective need.*

____ 5. Americans all have the same *wants.*

____ 6. *People-made resources* include tools and factories.

____ 7. Sometimes a *people-made resource* can be a *physical need.*

____ 8. Adam Smith was the father of modern economics.

____ 9. The most important resource is human labor.

____ 10. It is likely that in the future, all people's needs and wants will be met and there will be no more need to study economics.

____ 11. All of the side effects of progress are good.

____ 12. In economics, *scarcity* means there are fewer than five of a certain product in the world.

____ 13. Goods can be scarce for one person but not for another person.

____ 14. Most resources have only one possible use.

____ 15. An *economic tradeoff* involves choosing between different uses for a particular resource.

CHAPTER 2

FOUR ECONOMIC QUESTIONS

What Are the Four Basic Economic Questions?

Every society must answer four basic economic questions:

- **What** goods and services will be produced?
- **How** will these goods and services be produced?

- **How Much** (or **How Many**) will be produced?
- **Who** will get what is produced?

The answers to these four economic questions affect the life and the standard of living of every person in the society.

The Four Basic Economic Questions

1. **WHAT** will be produced?

2. **HOW** will it be produced?

3. **HOW MANY** will be produced?

4. **WHO** gets what is produced?

Figure 2–1 *The answers to the four basic economic questions affect how everyone in a society lives.*

What? questions deal with what outputs will be produced or consumed:

What will a farmer grow—wheat or orange trees?

What will factories make—machinery or consumer goods?

What will tax money be spent for—education or space exploration?

How? questions deal with how outputs are produced and how resources are used.

How will the farmer plow a field—with a horse-drawn plow or with a gasoline-powered tractor?

How will the farmer control pests—with organic farming methods or with chemical pesticides?

How will electricity be produced—by coal-powered plants or by nuclear plants?

How will clothing be sewn—by hand or by machine?

How Much? and **How Many?** questions deal with how much or how many resources will be used. They also deal with how fast resources will be used up.

How many trees in a forest will be cut for lumber? All of them? Or will some be left standing?

—If some trees are not cut, less lumber will be produced. But there will also be less soil erosion. Trees will continue to grow in the forest. Lumber can be produced in years to come as well as now.

Who? questions deal with the distribution of output. Who? questions are affected by the cost of goods and services.

Who gets what is produced? Only those who can pay? Only those who work?

—What about people who are too young, too old, too sick or disabled to work?

—What about people who can't find a job?

The way in which any one of these four questions is answered affects all of the other questions.

Alternative Costs

Every time an economic decision is made, something is chosen and something is given up. Whatever is given up is called the **alternative cost** or the **opportunity cost**.

> ❖ *Alternative cost = what is given up when a scarce resource is used in a certain way*

For example, you want to paint two rooms in your house or apartment. But you have only enough paint for one room. You must choose which room to paint.

No matter what you decide, you will have to give up something. The something you give up is your alternative cost.

If you paint the bedroom, the alternative cost is an unpainted kitchen. If you paint the kitchen, your alternative cost is an unpainted bedroom.

A 5-acre tract of land can be used in many ways. For example, it can be used for a park, a factory, a housing subdivision, or a shopping mall. But the same tract of land can only be used for one of these things.

—If the land is used for a shopping mall, it cannot be used for a park, a factory, or a housing subdivision. These alternatives must be given up.

—If the land is used for a shopping mall, the alternative cost for this shopping mall will be all the uses that are given up.

All economic decisions require trade-offs. Every economic decision has an alternative cost. The alternative cost is the *real* cost of every economic decision.

To make a good economic decision, all alternative costs must be compared. A good economic decision is the one with the smallest alternative cost.

Economic Choices of Producers

In an economy like that of the United States, many economic decisions are made by producers. For example, a car manufacturer must decide such questions as:

- What kind of cars will be made?
- How many cars will be made every year?
- How much will the cars cost?

The Reliable Car Company is planning next year's cars. The company can make a small number of very expensive cars. Or, it can make a large number of less expensive cars.

—If the company makes a small number of expensive cars, only a few rich people can buy Reliable cars. The alternative cost is less expensive cars for many people.

—If the company makes many less expensive cars, more people can buy Reliable cars. Then the alternative cost is the expensive cars that the company does not make.

The car company's decision is an economic decision. Whatever the company does *not* make is its alternative cost.

Another economic question that businesses must answer is:

- How will the business use its profits?

The Reliable Car Company could use its profits for any of the following:

—to buy more up-to-date machinery.

—to build a larger plant so that more cars can be produced.

— OR —

—to pay the company's stockholders (owners) larger dividends.

—to pay the factory workers higher wages.

If Reliable has large profits, it may be able to do all of these things.
If the company's profits are low, the company must choose which things it will do.

The alternative cost is whatever the company does *not* do with its profits. If the company chooses to buy new machinery and pay larger dividends and higher wages but not build a new plant, the unbuilt new plant is its alternative cost.

Economic Conflict

Economic decisions are based on values, beliefs, and opinions as well as on facts. The decision in any one case depends on *who* makes the decision and *what is important* to the decision maker.

For example, the 5-acre tract of land mentioned above in the discussion of alternative costs could be used several ways.

- One group of people wants a park.
- Another group wants a factory.
- Another group believes the land should be used for houses.

The final decision depends on which group has the power to decide.

Because economic decisions are based on values, beliefs, and opinions, these decisions often involve conflict between the people who control resources and those who have no control over resources.

Economic choices are made by consumers, by business and industry, and by

governments. Decisions by any one group affect decisions of the other groups.

Examples of economic questions that often cause conflict are:

- How much will factory workers be paid?

  —Workers want higher wages than employers want to pay them.

- What will be done with a wilderness area?

  —Conservationists want the area protected.
  —The state highway department wants to build a road through the wilderness area.
  —A logging company wants to cut the trees for lumber.

Settling Economic Conflicts

Two ways in which economic conflicts may be settled are:

- Market bargaining
- Government actions

Market bargaining refers to the way economic conflicts are settled by the way

people buy and sell goods and services. Market bargaining happens in many different ways. Consumers, workers, and businesses all use market bargaining.

Consumers use market bargaining when they:

- Buy Brand A because it is better quality than brand B.
- Refuse to buy Brand X because the price is too high.
- Refuse to go to a certain restaurant because the service is poor.

Workers use market bargaining when they:

- Organize labor unions.
- Bargain with employers for higher wages.
- Go on strike.
- Go to work someplace else.

Businesses use market bargaining when they:

- Offer benefits to workers to prevent strikes.
- Give consumers discount coupons.
- Reduce the price on an item.

Government actions are another way that economic conflicts may be settled. Here are some examples:

- State and federal lawmakers make rules for many economic decisions. For instance:
    - A law passed by Congress sets the minimum wage.
    - The Pure Food and Drug Act requires true labels on foods.
- Courts settle conflicts over property and contracts.
- The Constitution protects people's right to own property.

Think About It

1. Name the four basic economic questions that societies must answer. Give one example of each.
2. What is meant by an *alternative cost?*
3. Give one example of economic conflict.
4. Give one example of how market bargaining is used to work out economic conflict.
5. Find an example of economic conflict in your local newspaper. How might this conflict be solved?

End of Chapter Quiz

Answer True (T) or False (F):

_____ 1. The four basic economic questions every society must answer involve *what, how, how much,* and *who.*

_____ 2. *What* questions involve what people will do with goods that are produced.

_____ 3. *How* questions involve how goods and services will be produced.

_____ 4. "How many cars will be produced?" is an example of a *how much* question.

_____ 5. *Who* questions involve who will produce cars and who will produce TVs.

_____ 6. In every society, the government decides the answers to the four basic economic questions.

_____ 7. All economic decisions involve *tradeoffs.*

_____ 8. *Alternative costs* are what is given up when a scarce resource is used in one way and not in another.

_____ 9. If a company buys better machinery instead of buying more land, the machinery is its *alternative cost.*

_____ 10. If factory workers want higher wages than employers want to pay them, the result is *economic conflict.*

_____ 11. In our society, economic choices and decisions are made by consumers, by business and industry, and by government.

_____ 12. If you tell your friends not to eat at a certain restaurant because the waiters are rude, you are using a form of *market bargaining.*

_____ 13. Discount coupons from the local grocery store are an example of *market bargaining.*

_____ 14. The minimum wage set by Congress is an example of a government action to help settle economic conflicts.

_____ 15. People's right to own property is protected by the U.S. Constitution.

CHAPTER 3

ECONOMIC SYSTEMS

Every country has an **economic system**—that is, a way of making economic choices and decisions. Which system a country follows depends on:

- Who owns and controls the basic resources needed to produce goods and services.
- Who makes the basic economic decisions.

There are three basic types of economic systems. They are:

- Traditional Economies
- Command Economies
- Market Economies

1. TRADITIONAL AND COMMAND ECONOMIES

Traditional Economies

The economies of very simple societies are sometimes called **traditional economies.**

In a traditional economy, economic decisions are based on custom and tradition. Things are done today the way they have always been done. Land, tools, and equipment are owned by families or tribes. Children learn job skills from their parents. The same goods and services are produced generation after generation.

Here are some advantages of a traditional economy:

- A traditional economy is very stable. People know what to expect.
- Everyone has a place in the economy. No one is left out.

Here are some disadvantages:

- Individuals don't have much choice in the type of work they do. Their roles are based on custom.
- Change comes very slowly.

Today, traditional economies are common only among small agricultural societies in Latin America, Asia, and Africa.

Command Economies

As civilizations grew up in Egypt, in China, and in other places, their rulers wanted to increase their wealth. To do this, they needed to protect their people's food supply, to promote trade and growth, to defend themselves, and to make war on other countries. So they took control of the economy as well as the government of their state.

An economic system in which the decisions are made by a central authority like a king, a dictator, or a powerful political party is called a **command economy.**

In a command economy, land and capital goods are owned and controlled by the central authority. The central decision makers, also called planners, decide what will be produced, how it will be produced, how much will be produced, and how it will be distributed. Individuals are expected to follow the decisions of the central planners.

The ancient examples of command economies were societies built on agriculture. A more recent example of a command economy in an industrial society was the Soviet Union.

Here are some advantages of a command economy:

- Changes in what is produced, how it is produced, and how much is produced can be made fairly quickly.
- The needs of the entire country can be considered by the central planners.
  - If a country's major need is food, planners can organize the country's production resources to increase the food supply.
  - If the major need is industrial growth, the country's production resources can be organized to meet that need.

Here are some disadvantages:

- Individuals are not encouraged to develop new ideas.
- Individuals have few incentives to work hard.
- The needs and wants of individuals are not always met.
- Day-to-day decision-making is sometimes very slow because a large number of people, called a **bureaucracy**, are involved in making decisions.
- Power is kept in the hands of a few people—nobles or a single political party—who often abuse the power for their own benefit.

2. MARKET ECONOMIES

The **market economy** (also called **capitalism** or the **private enterprise system**) is the result of the millions of buying and selling decisions made by millions of individuals. No one runs the economy. It runs itself.

The U.S. economy, as well as most other modern-day economies, is basically a market economy.

What Is a Market?

Why do we call this kind of an economy a **market** economy? Traditionally, a *market* is a place where people buy and sell things. An example is a farmers' market, where you can buy vegetables directly from farmers. But for economists, the word *market* means something slightly different. It refers to the *actions* of buying and selling, not just to the place where things are bought and sold. A market can exist even if the buyers and sellers never meet—for example, a mail-order business.

A market is made up of **people** and **actions**.

- The **people** in a market are all the buyers and sellers of a product or service.

- The **action** of a market is buying and selling, that is, exchanging a product or service for money.

A grocery store is a market. So is a shoe repair shop, a movie theater, or a gas station. So are kids selling cookies at a bake sale. In each of these markets, buyers exchange money for a product or service.

The Beginnings of Market Economies

The idea of a market economy started about 200 years ago, during the Industrial Revolution in 18th-century England. This was the time when goods began to be made in factories with large machines powered by steam or water, instead of being made by hand.

As individual inventors, industrialists, and entrepreneurs became wealthy, they also became more powerful in government. They were not satisfied with an economic system that was designed to benefit the nobles, kings, and landowners. They wanted an economic system that would benefit them.

PROFILE

ADAM SMITH
THE FATHER OF ECONOMICS

ADAM SMITH (1723-1790), sometimes called "the father of economics," explained the ideas of a market economy in a book titled *The Wealth of Nations.*

Smith believed that a nation's wealth was measured by what its entrepreneurs and its work force produced. He believed that the way for a nation to become wealthy was for its workers and businesses to produce and sell whatever they wanted, and as much as they wanted. Businesses should be as productive and efficient as possible. He believed that people's desire to make a profit would naturally encourage them to make sensible economic decisions.

Smith knew that producers want a high price for what they sell, while consumers want to pay a low price for what they buy. Workers want high wages, but employers want to pay low wages. Smith believed that if all these groups bargained freely, they would reach a compromise that would be in the best interest of everyone.

Competition in the marketplace would keep prices fair. Buyers would show producers what was most profitable to produce. Efficient businesses would do well. Inefficient businesses would fail.

Smith believed that when consumers and businesses worked for their own self interest, all of society would benefit. The economy would run smoothly, as if it were guided by an **invisible hand.** In other words, Smith believed that what was economically good for individuals and businesses would also be good for the nation's economy.

Smith believed that government's only role in the economy was to keep monopolies and special interests from interfering with competition and the natural growth of the economy. The invisible hand, not the government, would guide the economy.

❖ **Entrepreneurs** = *People who take an economic risk to create something new, such as starting a new business or introducing a new product*

Economic Decisions in a Market Economy

Economic decisions in a pure market economy are made by buyers and sellers in the marketplace. Land and capital goods—factories, tools, etc.—are privately owned.

A market economy depends on a specialized industrialized society in which—

- Most individuals cannot meet their own material needs,
- People must work because they need money,
- People meet most of their material needs by buying goods and services with money, and
- Buyers and sellers compete in the marketplace, each working for his or her own best interests.

The Flow of Money in a Market Economy

A **market economy** is really made up of two markets: a **resource market** and a **product market.** In each of these two markets, something is exchanged between producers and individuals.

In the **resource market**, the resources that producers need (labor, land, capital goods) are exchanged for money (wages, rent, interest, and profits). Individuals provide resources to producers. Producers in turn provide money to individuals. The diagram below shows how this works.

Producers pay—

- *wages* in exchange for labor,
- *rent* in exchange for land,
- *interest* on borrowed money (bonds), and
- *profits* (or *dividends*) to individuals who invest money (such as in stocks) and thus become part-owners of the business.

Figure 3–1 ▶
The Resource Market

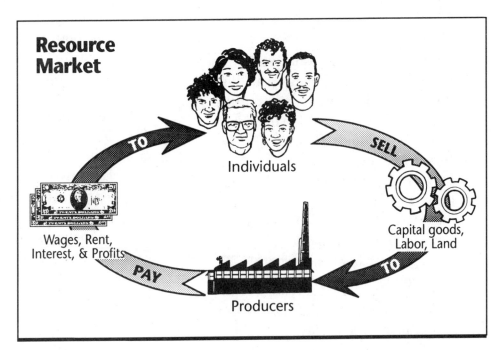

Resource Market

Individuals

Capital goods, Labor, Land

Wages, Rent, Interest, & Profits

Producers

Figure 3–2 ▶
The Product Market

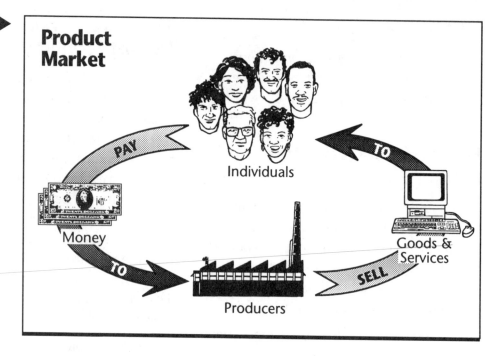

Product Market

PAY

Individuals

TO

Money

Goods & Services

TO

SELL

Producers

In the **product market,** products and services are exchanged for money. Producers provide products and services to individuals. Individuals in turn provide money to producers in payment for the products and services.

The diagram above shows how this works.

The resource and product markets are related.

- Businesses use the resources (land, labor, and capital goods) that they buy from individuals to produce goods and services which they then sell to individuals.
- Businesses use the money they receive in payment for these goods and services to pay individuals wages, rent, interest, and profits.
- Individuals use the money they earn in wage, rent, interest, and profits to buy more goods and services.

Figure 3–3 shows the circular flow of money in a market economy.

Advantages and Disadvantages of a Market Economy

A market economy has a number of advantages:

- Large numbers of people are involved in making economic decisions.
- Individuals are free to decide on and work for their own best interests.
- Producers are free to produce what they wish in the way that they wish.
- Individuals are encouraged to develop new ideas and technologies. This helps to create a wide variety of goods and services.
- The economy is flexible and able to change to meet people's needs.
- People are free to choose what type of work they wish to do.
- Consumers are free to buy the goods and services they choose.

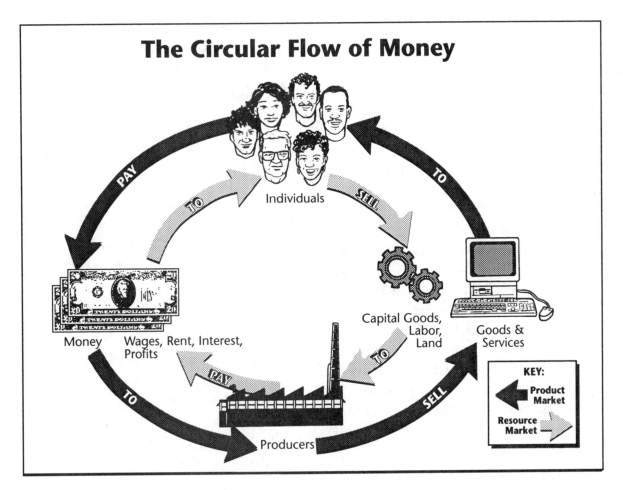

The Circular Flow of Money

Individuals

Money   Wages, Rent, Interest, Profits

Capital Goods, Labor, Land

Goods & Services

Producers

KEY:
Product Market
Resource Market

Figure 3–3 *The Circular Flow of Money*

A market economy also has a number of disadvantages:

- Individuals who are unable to work (those who are too young, too old, or too ill) have no way of meeting their own needs.
- There is no guarantee that individuals will succeed in their business or work. Those who fail may suffer harsh consequences.
- The needs of society as a whole are often overlooked. If individuals work only for their own interests, the good of society may suffer. Air and water pollution are examples.
- The economy is subject to ups and downs called **business cycles.** The down parts of the cycle hurt everyone.

- The market economy exploits labor.

These last two disadvantages are discussed more fully below.

Two Special Disadvantages of a Market Economy: Business Cycles and Exploitation of Labor

Economists measure how well a country's economy is doing by keeping track of the total value of goods and services. This total value is called the **Gross National Product (GNP).** In boom times, the GNP grows. Business is good. Most workers have jobs. Businesses make a profit.

But boom times don't go on forever. Economic growth reaches a peak and then slows down. When a business slowdown lasts for two quarters (six months), it is called a **recession**. If it goes on for a long time, or if it is really bad, it is called a **depression**. Less money is invested in new production. Profits go down. Businesses fail. Workers are laid off and cannot find other work. People cannot pay their bills. Everyone is hurt.

These economic ups-and-downs are called **business cycles.** Sometimes it takes many years for better times to return.

Market economies have another important disadvantage. In a market economy, workers sell their labor in return for wages. But individual workers are too weak to bargain for high wages against powerful businesses. As a result, in a pure market economy, workers are paid very low wages by their employers. By paying low wages, business owners in a pure market economy make a lot of money and exploit their workers. This was the situation in the 1800s.

> ❖ *Exploit* = To take selfish and unfair advantage of someone

Modern market economies have been able to partly overcome the problem of low pay. Workers have combined into unions and have forced businesses to pay better wages. And democratic governments have passed laws that have stopped some of the worst exploitation of workers by business owners.

Modern market economies have been less successful in controlling business cycles. No one can predict when a recession or depression will occur or how bad it will be. Governments do give some help to people who are hurt in a recession or depression, but often it is not enough.

3. COMMUNISM: A NEW KIND OF COMMAND ECONOMY

The two special disadvantages of market economies—depressions and the exploitation of labor—bothered many thinkers on economics in the 1800s. Many of them felt that only a revolution would cure these ills. But no successful revolution against capitalism took place until the twentieth century, in Russia.

Communism in the Soviet Union

In the early 1900s, Russia was ruled by an emperor called the czar. The major Russian cities were industrialized, but the country as a whole lagged far behind other industrialized nations. Most Russian people were poor, uneducated peasants.

World War I brought about the collapse of this system. The Russians were badly defeated by the Germans. Russia's industry and agriculture were disrupted, and its economy was in ruins. The Russian people revolted against the czar. One political party gained control of the government. This was the Communist Party, which followed the ideas of the German economist Karl Marx *(see box)*. A Soviet (council) government was set up, and political power was gradually concentrated in the hands of central Communist Party leaders.

In order to help the Soviet Union catch up with other industrialized countries, government leaders took over economic decisions. Central planners organized the economy to develop heavy industries. Until a basic industrial system was devel-

PROFILE

KARL MARX
THE FATHER OF COMMUNISM

KARL MARX (1818-1883), lived in the 19th century. He was a German, although he lived more than half of his life in England. In Marx's time there were no strong unions, and governments did little or nothing to help people who were exploited by their employers or who lost their jobs during business downturns.

Marx felt that it was unfair for a few people (those who controlled the raw materials, factories, and machines) to get rich from the work of everyone else. He believed that everyone deserved decent housing, enough food, an education, good health care, and the right to self-

determination. Marx's most important work was the 3-volume *Das Kapital* ("Capital"). In it he predicted that the disadvantages of the capitalist system would weaken it, and that the workers would finally rise up and overthrow it.

Marx favored a return to a command economy, but this time one for the benefit of the workers, not the rulers. In his ideal economic system, all property would be owned jointly by all the people. Everyone would be equal in power, wealth, and rights, and no one would be exploited.

Marx called his economic system **communism.** However, Marx's ideal communist system is very different from communism as it developed in the Soviet Union and China. ◄

oped, the country could not produce the things other industrialized countries already had, such as cars and consumer goods. Except in agriculture, private property and private enterprise were not allowed. Farmers, however, were allowed to grow and sell produce from their own private gardens.

The Soviet Union concentrated on building its military strength. After World War II, it put Communist governments in power in most of the countries of Eastern Europe. But Soviet-style Communism did not work out the way Marx had intended. In every Communist nation, food and housing were scarce. Consumer goods lacked variety and were of poor quality.

High officials of the Communist Party lived well, while powerful secret police systems kept everybody else in line.

Similar Communist systems were set up in China and other Asian countries controlled or influenced by the Soviet Union after World War II. By 1980, over one-third of the world's population lived under a Communist regime.

The Collapse of European Communist Regimes: 1989–1991

By the end of the 1980s, the failures of Communist governments made people rise up against this economic system.

People's revolts destroyed Communist governments in Eastern Europe. In the Soviet Union, pressures against the Communist system increased, and the system finally collapsed. In 1991 the Soviet Union itself was dissolved.

Communism did not collapse in Asia. In China, in the 1970s and 1980s, some kinds of private enterprise were permitted. But a student revolt against the government in 1989 was put down, and the Chinese Communist government stayed in power.

4. SOCIALISM AND MIXED ECONOMIES

Socialism

Socialism is based on the ideas of Marx and other critics of capitalism. It is similar to Communism in some ways. Socialism supports public ownership of industry. It believes that central planning is needed to protect the interest of all the people. It also believes that most of the nation's wealth should not be in the hands of only a few people.

The major difference between socialism and Communism is that socialist governments are democratic. There is no all-powerful political party, no dictators, and no secret police.

Socialist ideas are part of the economic system in several Western European nations today. Great Britain and Sweden are two examples. In these countries, public utilities, transportation, and medical services are **nationalized.** That is, they are publicly owned and operated by the government.

However, most industry in Great Britain and Sweden is privately owned, just as in capitalist countries. The government controls part of the economy to protect the welfare of all its citizens. These countries are sometimes called **capitalist-welfare** states.

Modern Mixed Economies

In the industrial nations, pure command and pure market economies do not exist today. All industrial nations now have a combination of market and command economies called **mixed economies**.

The United States has a mixed economic system. It has the basic features of a market economy, but it is not a pure market system. Government regulates some parts of the economy. You will learn more about the U.S. economic system in the next chapter of this book.

Think About It

1. Give two advantages and two disadvantages of a traditional economy.
2. Give two advantages and two disadvantages of a command economy.
3. Give two advantages and two disadvantages of a market economy.
4. What is a *mixed economy?*

End of Chapter Quiz

Answer True (T) or False (F):

____ 1. *Traditional economies* are very stable, and the rules of the society and roles of the citizens change very slowly.

____ 2. About half of the countries in the world today have traditional economies.

____ 3. Individual people decide what will be produced in a *command economy.*

____ 4. In a command economy changes in what is produced and how much is produced can be made fairly quickly.

____ 5. In a command economy the needs of the entire country can be considered.

____ 6. The United States today has a command economy.

____ 7. A *market* must include a building where goods are bought and sold.

____ 8. The action of a market is producing goods.

____ 9. In a *market economy*, people work for wages and buy goods and services with money.

____ 10. In a market economy, producers are told by the government what they must produce.

____ 11. An *entrepreneur* is a person who takes an economic risk such as starting a new business.

____ 12. Adam Smith believed that a market economy would run itself with an invisible hand.

____ 13. In a market economy, the needs of all citizens are met.

____ 14. In a market economy, people are free to choose what work they do.

____ 15. Karl Marx wrote about an economic system that he called *communism* in which everyone would be equal in power, wealth, and rights.

____ 16. To *exploit* means to take selfish and unfair advantage of someone.

____ 17. Socialism is an economic system in which some industries, such as transportation and utilities, are publicly owned.

____ 18. A *mixed economy* is the same thing as a *market economy.*

CHAPTER 4

THE U.S. ECONOMIC SYSTEM

U.S. Capitalism

You learned in Chapter 3 that the United States has a *mixed economy*. It has many features of a market economy, along with some government regulations. However, the U.S. economic system is basically a **private enterprise,** or **capitalist, system.** This means that most of the resources needed to produce goods and services are privately owned.

> ❖ **Capitalism** = *An economic system in which the resources needed for production are privately owned*
>
> ❖ **Financial capital,** *or simply* **Capital** = *Money used to pay for capital goods*
>
> ❖ **Capitalists** = *Owners of the resources that are needed for production and manufacturing, such as factories and machinery*
>
> ❖ **Capital goods** = *People-made resources, such as factories, machines, and tools*

Who Are Capitalists?

Capitalists are those individuals who own capital (money) and capital goods. They control investment and production decisions.

Capitalists make up a very small percentage of the U.S. population. In the United States, about 18 out of every 1,000 adults in the work force owns or controls a business with 10 or more employees.

The top 10% of families in the United States own more than two-thirds of the nation's wealth. More than one-third of the nation's wealth belongs to the top 1% of U.S. families.

1. MARKET ECONOMY FEATURES OF U.S. CAPITALISM

U.S. capitalism has many of the features of a market economy including:

- Private property
- Economic freedom
- Voluntary exchanges
- The profit motive

Private Property

Most property in the U.S. is owned by private individuals or by businesses that are owned by private individuals. This includes land, personal property, business property, and money. People may buy, sell, and use their property as they wish. People may also make contracts.

❖ **Contracts** = *Formal agreements about the use or sale of property or labor*

Economic Freedom

In the United States, both producers and workers have economic freedom. Producers may produce whatever products and services they wish. Workers may choose whatever jobs they wish.

Individuals are free to own their own businesses, although not many do. Only 8% of the population are self-employed in non-farm businesses.

Producers and workers are also free to compete in the marketplace. Competition encourages fair prices, efficiency, and new ideas.

Voluntary Exchange

Producers are free to sell their products and services for the price they wish. Consumers are free to buy or refuse to buy products and services as they wish.

Consumers influence the price of goods as they decide what price they are willing to pay.

The Profit Motive

Individuals are free to act in their own best interests in the U.S. economic system. This is called the **profit motive.**

Producers are free to sell products and services at the highest price they can get. Consumers are free to shop for the lowest price they can find. Workers are free to bargain for higher wages and better working conditions. Individuals are free to save or invest money in order to earn interest or profits.

Figure 4–1 Profit Motive in Action

31

2. GOVERNMENT AND THE U.S. ECONOMY

The federal government has many important roles in the U.S. economy. It acts as—

- Protector of—
  —private property
  —free competition
  —savers and investors
  —consumers
  —workers
- Provider of public goods and services
- Helper in dealing with the nation's economic problems by—
  —taxing
  —spending
  —regulating the money supply
  —promoting economic well-being

Government as Protector

Protecting Private Property

In the United States a citizen's right to own property is protected by law. Even the government itself cannot take privately owned property unless it has a good reason and pays a fair price for the property.

Protecting Free Competition

In the United States competition is protected by law. Unfair trade practices that would interfere with free competition are forbidden. If a company gets so big and powerful that it controls the market and stops competition, the government can step in.

This happened to the telephone company in the 1970s. One company, the American Telephone and Telegraph company, used to control nearly all the telephone lines and telephone equipment in the United States. The government forced it to break up into many smaller companies and allowed other telephone companies that compete with each other to grow.

Protecting Savers and Investors

Federal laws and rules made by federal agencies regulate banks and savings institutions to protect savers and investors. Deposits in banks and savings institutions are insured by the Federal Deposit Insurance Corporation (FDIC) or the Federal Savings and Loan Insurance Corporation (FSLIC).

Companies that sell securities to investors are regulated by the Securities and Exchange Commission (SEC). These companies must register with the SEC and also provide a data sheet about their company for investors. To guard against fraud, the SEC makes rules for buying and selling securities. It also requires stock exchanges and brokers to have licenses.

Protecting Consumers

Federal laws and regulations make rules about the safety of many products, from food and drugs, to clothing and toys, to automobiles. For example, automobiles must have certain safety equipment such as seat belts and pollution control devices.

Federal, state, and local governments hire consumer safety inspectors to check various products. A consumer injured by an unsafe product can take the manufacturer to court.

Fair practices in advertising and sales are the responsibility of the Federal Trade Commission and the Federal Communications Commission.

Local governments have building codes to ensure that buildings are safe.

Protecting Workers

The government makes laws to protect workers. A person's right to have a job regardless of sex, religion, or race is protected by federal law. Workers who are harassed or discriminated against on the job because of their sex or race may take their case to court.

A minimum wage is set by federal law. Safety rules for work places are the responsibility of the Occupational Safety and Health Administration (OSHA).

Labor unions are protected by law. Employers cannot fire workers just because they belong to a union.

Providing Public Goods and Services

Many public services are provided by local governments. Some of these are education, libraries, hospitals, police and fire protection, streets and bridges, sewers and garbage collection.

State governments also provide services such as education, hospitals, and highways.

Some of the public services that the federal government is responsible for are running the national parks and national forests, the national defense, providing benefits and services to veterans.

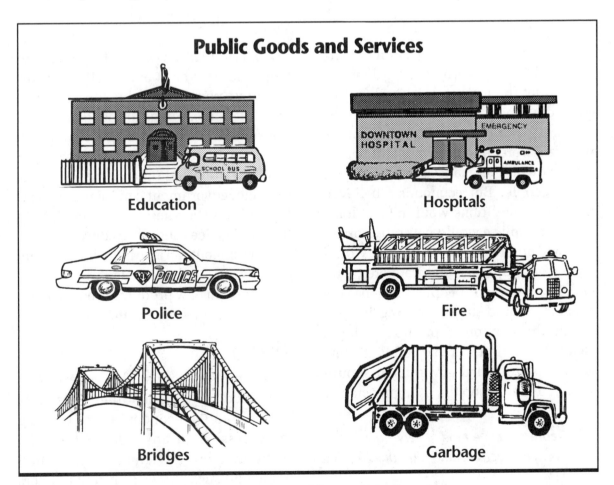

Public Goods and Services

Education

Hospitals

Police

Fire

Bridges

Garbage

Figure 4–2 *The U.S. Government provides public goods and services*

PROFILE

JOHN MAYNARD KEYNES
THE FATHER OF KEYNESIAN ECONOMICS

JOHN MAYNARD KEYNES (1883-1946), a British economist, wrote a book called *The General Theory of Employment, Interest, and Money* (1936) that called for more government involvement in capitalist economies. Keynes believed that government should watch out for the well-being of all its citizens.

He felt that it was government's duty to take direct action in hard times to keep the economy stable and to regulate its growth.

In times of high unemployment, Keynes said, government should provide jobs for workers who can't find work in private businesses. Also, government should use its powers to tax and spend to help keep the economy stable. In particular, he believed that government should lower taxes during depressions. ◄

Dealing with Economic Problems

Until the Great Depression of the 1930s, the U.S. government's policy had been to let the marketplace work out its own solutions to economic problems.

During periods of recession, many workers were unemployed and wages went down. This caused hardships for many people. But economists believed that these conditions wouldn't last long. The marketplace would naturally correct its own problems. Lower wages would encourage employers to hire more workers. Then as more people had jobs, the economy would start to grow again.

But the economic problems of the Great Depression were so bad that some economists decided government should step in to help keep the economy stable.

❖ **Depression** = A time of very slow economic activity and high unemployment

Taxing

Government can raise or lower taxes to help stabilize the economy. When taxes are low, people and businesses have more of their earnings to spend or invest. Consumers can buy more goods and services. Business can hire more workers.

When prices go up and inflation gets too high, government can increase taxes. If people and businesses have less money to spend, prices should go down.

Government can also help the economy grow by offering lower taxes to businesses that invest in new production equipment. These are called **tax incentives.**

Spending

During recessions, the government may increase its spending. This puts money into the economy to try to bring the recession to an end. To help the economy grow, government may spend money on such things as hiring workers and building airports, roads, bridges, and other public works.

Keynes believed that in bad economic times it was government's duty to help the economy even if government had to borrow money to do so. Borrowing money to pay for increased spending is called **deficit spending.**

The total amount of money that the government owes is called the **national debt.** Since the 1980s, the national debt has grown rapidly. Today it is well over 4.5 trillion dollars—about $18,000 for every man, woman, and child in the United States. The federal government now spends more money to pay interest on the national debt than it spends for education, social services, health, and Medicare all put together.

Regulating the Money Supply

Another way that government works to keep the economy stable is to regulate the money supply. This is the job of the **Federal Reserve System** (usually called the **Fed** for short). You will learn more about the Fed in Chapter 18.

If the Fed increases the money supply when the nation's economy slows down. People are encouraged to spend more and help the economy grow. If the nation's economy is growing too fast, the Fed may lower the money supply in an effort to hold down inflation.

❖ **Inflation** = A continuing rise in prices

Promoting Economic Well-Being

In a market economy, products and services are distributed according to people's ability to pay. However, all people do not earn money, so some are unable to provide for their own material needs. In particular, this includes the very young without families who can care for them, the very old, those who are too ill or disabled to work, those who have no job skills, and those who cannot find work because of problems in the economy.

Certain government programs are designed to distribute a portion of the nation's goods and services to these groups that are left out of a market economy.

Aid to Families with Dependent Children (AFDC) provides money to poor families with children. Social Security provides money to elderly and disabled people. Medicare and Medicaid provide medical care to elderly, disabled, and poor people. Food stamps are another benefit to low-income people. Unemployment insurance provides short-term help for some workers who have lost their job.

Billions of dollars of government money also go to private businesses each year. Price supports and low-interest loans go to farmers. In order to keep the price of certain agricultural products from falling too low, some farmers are also paid not to grow that crop.

Economic Goals

The U.S. economic system is shaped by the activities of many groups of people. Economic groups in the United States include employers, workers, and consumers; families, businesses, and government agencies. All of these groups take part in producing, selling, and buying goods and services. All of these groups and activities together form the U.S. economic system.

Each group in the U.S. economic system has its own economic goals. Workers' goals are jobs, good wages, and a decent standard of living. Consumers want quality products, low prices, and a good standard of living. Business wants to make a profit. All groups want to be treated fairly, to share in economic benefits, and to be protected from economic hardships such as poverty, unemployment, bank failures, and business failures.

A list of U.S. economic goals might include freedom, efficiency, justice, security, stability, and growth.

- If the economic system is **free**, consumers, workers, and producers can make their own economic decisions.
- If the economic system is **efficient**, economic resources will be used in the way that will produce the most goods and services.
- If the economic system is **just**, all people will be treated fairly and will share its costs and benefits in an equal way.
- If the economic system is **secure**, people will be protected from economic hardships.
- If the economic system is **stable**, workers will have jobs and prices will be stable.
- If the economy is **growing**, people will be able to improve their standard of living.

Economic Problems

Some economic groups in the United States today have a lot of decision-making power. Other groups have very little. Some groups have a lot of control over the nation's resources. Other groups have very little control over the nation's resources.

Some people in the United States today are very well off. Others are very poor. Almost all the needs and wants of some people are satisfied. Few of the needs and wants of some other people are satisfied.

The United States today is troubled by many economic problems and conflicts. Homeless people need housing. Unemployed workers need jobs. Taxpayers want lower taxes. Air and water pollution are getting worse, yet the costs of cleanup will be very great.

A major economic problem today is getting rid of poverty and protecting the environment at the same time. This problem can be solved only if people understand how the economic system works.

Studying the U.S. economic system can help you understand—

- How the economy is organized,
- How economic decisions are made,
- How the system provides for people's material needs and wants.

Think About It

1. What is *capitalism*? Who are *capitalists*?
2. Why is the U.S. economic system called a *mixed economy*? Explain.
3. Name three things that government does to help solve economic problems.
4. Name three ways in which government acts as a protector in the economy of the United States.
5. Name two important goals of the U.S. economic system.
6. Name one major economic problem in the United States today. Why is it a problem? What solution do you think might solve this problem?

End of Chapter Quiz

Answer True (T) or False (F):

_____ 1. The United States has a *mixed economy*. That means it has many features of a market economy plus some government regulations.

_____ 2. *Capitalism* is an economic system in which resources needed for production are owned by the government.

_____ 3. *Capitalists* include workers but not factory owners.

_____ 4. Capitalists make up about half of the U.S. population.

_____ 5. Most property, including businesses, money, and land, in the United States is owned by private individuals.

_____ 6. A formal agreement to sell property is called a *contract*.

_____ 7. The profit *motive* is a feature of U.S. capitalism that allows business owners to sell products at the highest price they can get.

_____ 8. Because the United States has a free enterprise economic system the government is not allowed to make any laws to protect workers or consumers.

_____ 9. Education is an important service provided by the U.S. government.

_____ 10. John Maynard Keynes believed that government should never interfere in the economy, no matter how much unemployment there was.

_____ 11. A *depression* is a time of rapid economic growth.

_____ 12. Giving certain *tax incentives* to businesses is one way government tries to encourage businesses to invest in new production equipment and hire more people.

_____ 13. The *Federal Reserve System* is the government agency that collects taxes.

_____ 14. *Inflation* means a continuing rise in prices.

_____ 15. The existence of homeless people in the United States today is an economic problem.

CHAPTER 5

DEMAND IN A MARKET ECONOMY

What is Demand?

In a market economy, answers to the economic questions *What will be produced?* and *How much will be produced?* are influenced by **demand.**

In Chapter 1 you read about wants and needs. But few people have enough money to buy all the things they want or need.

In economics, the term *demand* is used for how much of their wants and needs people are able and willing to buy at any one price.

> ❖ **Demand** = *The amount of goods or services that people want or need and that they are willing and able to buy at a given price*

Notice that demand has three conditions:

- Desire or need
- Willingness to pay
- Ability to pay

All three conditions must exist in order to have demand.

Consumers may need or want shoes or apples or TVs. How many apples or pairs of shoes or TVs consumers are able and willing to buy at a given price equals the demand for that product at a particular time.

The Law of Demand

The **law of demand** says that consumers will buy more of a product or service at a low price than they will buy at a high price. Employers will hire more workers at low wages than at high wages. In other words, *demand for goods and services, including labor, will go up as prices, including wages, go down.*

1. THE DEMAND FOR BICYCLES IN BARNSVILLE

Suppose that you own a bicycle store in the town of Barnsville. There are two other bike stores in town, but since bicycles are very popular in Barnsville, all three stores do a good business.

The *Sprint* is your most popular bike. The *Sprint* is also the best quality bike in its price range. How many *Sprints* should you order this year?

To help you answer this question you need to know the demand for *Sprints* in

Figure 5–1 ▶
*Demand for
the* Sprint
bicycle

Price per Bicycle	Number of Bicycles Demanded
$450	50
$400	100
$350	200
$300	500
$250	700

Barnsville. Figure 5–1 shows the estimated number of *Sprint* bicycles the people of Barnsville will buy at different prices. How many *Sprint* bicycles you sell will depend on what price you decide to charge.

The left-hand column in Figure 5–1 lists five possible prices for *Sprint* bicycles. The highest price ($450) is at the top of this column. As you read down the column, the prices get smaller.

The right-hand column in Figure 5–1 shows the number of bicycles demanded at each of the five prices. The smallest number (50) is at the top of this column. As you read down the column, the numbers get larger.

Notice that as the left-hand column goes from big to little, the right-hand column goes from little to big. As the price goes down, demand for *Sprints* goes up.

- *How many bicycles are demanded at the price of $350?*
  (Answer: 200 bicycles)

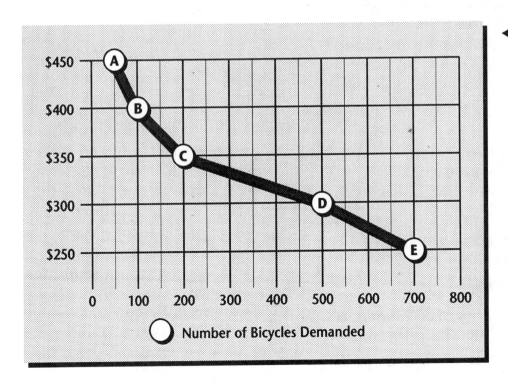

◀ **Figure 5–2**
*Demand
curve
graph for
Sprints*

Now let's look at these numbers another way. The graph in Figure 5–2 is a picture of the numbers in Figure 5–1.

The line on the graph in Figure 5–2 is called a **demand curve.** The demand curve shows the relationship between the price of *Sprint* bicycles and the number of *Sprints* demanded. The demand curve shows the **level of demand** at every price.

The horizontal (left to right) lines on the graph represent the different prices *Sprints* might sell for. The five different prices, ranging from $450 to $250, are printed on the left side of the graph. The highest price ($450) is at the top.

The vertical (up and down) lines on the graph show how many *Sprints* are demanded at each price. Five numbers are printed at the bottom of the graph. The lowest number of *Sprints* (50) demanded at any of these five prices is at the left.

Each dot on the graph shows the number of *Sprints* demanded at one particular price. For example, Dot A is printed where the $450 price line (horizontal line) meets the 50 quantity line (vertical line). **Dot A** shows that at $450 each, 50 *Sprint* bicycles are demanded. **Dot E** shows that at $250 each, 700 Sprints could be sold.

- *What does **Dot D** show?*
  (Answer: At $300 each,
  500 bicycles are demanded.)

Changes in the Number of Bicycles Demanded Based on Price

Notice how many more *Sprints* are demanded every time the price drops by $50. The price charged for each *Sprint*

makes a big difference in the number of *Sprints* demanded.

If you decide to charge $450 each, you can expect to sell only 50 *Sprints*. However, a drop in price of only $50 per bike causes demand to double (100). Dropping the price another $50 doubles the demand again (200). One more $50 drop in price (to $300) causes demand to jump to 500. At the lowest price listed, demand goes to 700.

Even though there is only a $200 difference between the highest and lowest price ($450 − $250 = $200), you can sell 14 times as many bikes (50 × 14 = 700) at the lowest price compared with the highest price. You would lose 650 sales (700 − 50 = 650) by raising your price from $250 to $450.

Price clearly has a major effect on the demand for *Sprints* in Barnsville. Demand that shows a major change as a result of a small price change is called **elastic demand.**

> ❖ *Elastic demand* = A major change in the amount of a product demanded that results from a small change in price

Competition from Substitute Products

Why is the demand for Sprints *elastic?*

One reason that the demand for *Sprints* is elastic is competition from the other bike shops in town that sell similar bikes. If another store sells a similar bike for a lower price, many customers won't pay a higher price for a *Sprint* even if it is a little bit better quality.

The numbers in Figure 5–3 show how many *Sprints* you would sell at each price if you were the only bike shop in town.

Figure 5–3 ▶
Demand for Sprints bicycles with no competition

Price per Bicycle	Number of Bicycles Demanded
$450	350
$400	500
$350	550
$300	600
$250	700

The prices listed in the left-hand column of Figure 5–3 are the same as those in Figure 5–1. Notice that there is a $50 difference between each price listed. In both charts, the number of *Sprints* demanded at the low price of $250 is 700.

But notice the difference in Column 2 of the charts. The number of bicycles demanded (right-hand column) at each of the other prices is higher in Figure 5–3 than in Figure 5–1. For example, with competition (Figure 5–1), the number of *Sprints* demanded at $300 is only 500. With no competition (Figure 5–3), 600 *Sprints* are demanded at $300.

With competition, only 200 *Sprints* are demanded at $350. With no competi-

tion, the number of *Sprints* demanded at $350 jumps to 550.

The $50 change in price causes a much smaller change in the number of *Sprints* demanded when there is no substitute product for customers to buy than when customers have a choice. Competition is a major factor in keeping prices low.

With or without competition, the difference between the highest price and the lowest price you might charge for a *Sprint* is $200 ($450 − $250 = $200). Figure 5–1 shows that with competition, you would lose 650 sales by raising your price from $250 to $450. Figure 5–3 shows that without competition you would lose only 350 sales by raising your price from $250 to $450.

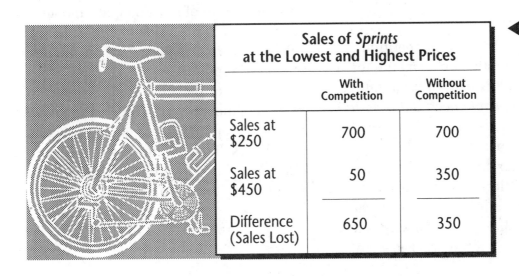

Sales of *Sprints* at the Lowest and Highest Prices		
	With Competition	Without Competition
Sales at $250	700	700
Sales at $450	50	350
Difference (Sales Lost)	650	350

◀ *Figure 5–4*
Sales of Sprints at the highest and lowest prices

Figure 5–5 ▶
Demand curve graph for Sprints with no competition

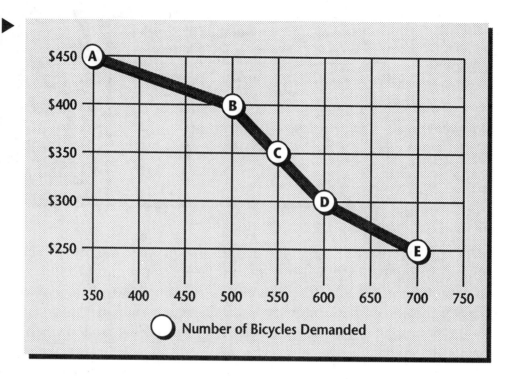

The demand curve in Figure 5–5 is a picture of the numbers in Figure 5–4.

Study the demand curves in Figure 5–5 and 5–2. Notice how much flatter the demand curve in Figure 5–5 is at higher prices compared with the demand curve in Figure 5–2.

A flat demand curve shows that price has less influence on demand for that product. A flat demand curve means that demand for that product is not elastic.

Necessity or Luxury?

Other things besides competition influence how elastic the demand for a product is. One of the most important is, *How much do people need the product? Is the product a necessity or a luxury?*

Demand for necessities is less elastic than demand for luxuries and is likely to change very little even if prices go up.

Bicycles are not a necessity. Many people who will buy a new bike at a low price will not buy if the price goes up.

Price of Product Compared to Income

If the price of a product is a large portion of a buyer's income, changes in the price of that product will have a major effect on its demand.

The price of a new car is a large portion of most people's income. An increase in the price of new cars is likely to have a major effect on the number of new cars demanded.

The price of a something like apples is a small portion of most people's income. An increase in the price of apples is not likely to have a major effect on the demand for apples.

The cost of bicycles is not as great a portion of most people's income as a new car. However, an increase in the price of bicycles is likely to have a significant effect on the demand for bicycles for people with low or moderate incomes.

Level of Demand

> ❖ *Level of demand = The total amount of a product that is demanded at all prices at any one time*

The total amount of a product demanded at each and every price changes over time.

At one time demand was high for horse-drawn carriages. People bought low-cost carriages, medium-cost carriages, and expensive carriages. At that time there was no demand for cars. In fact, cars did not even exist.

Today there is almost no demand for horse-drawn carriages at any price. Demand for cars has taken its place.

Many factors influence the level of demand for a product. When level of demand changes, more than one factor is probably at work. Some of the factors that influence the level of demand are:

- People's tastes—what people want
- How much money people have to spend
- How much money people expect to have in the future
- The price of substitute products
- How much satisfaction people get from the product
- How many people want the product

What People Want

The level of demand for a product shows how many people are able and willing to buy that product. When a certain product is in fashion, the level of demand is high. When people's tastes change, the level of demand for that product drops.

Businesses spend great sums of money for advertising in order to change people's minds about what they want to buy. By changing people's wants, businesses hope to increase the level of demand for their product.

Bicycle riding is very popular in Barnsville today. However, if other types of recreation become more popular in the future, the level of demand for bicycles could drop.

Bicycles are also an important means of transportation in Barnsville. If the town should grow much larger, distances might be too great for bicycling to be a satisfactory method of transportation. More people might want cars instead of bikes.

How Much Money People Have to Spend

The level of demand for non-essential products at each and every price goes up (or down) as the amount of money people have goes up (or down).

In good economic times people are likely to spend more on non-essential items like new bicycles. When people have less money to spend, they will use their old bikes and buy fewer new bikes.

People's Expectations for Their Future Income

Level of demand is influenced not only by how much money people have now but also by how much money people expect to have in the near future.

If people expect that their income will go down in the near future, they will probably stop spending for non-essential items such as new bikes.

The Cost of Substitute Products

> ❖ **Substitute product** = A product that can take the place of another product

The level of demand for some products is heavily influenced by the price and availability of substitute products.

The level of demand for leather belts may go down if vinyl belts are available at a lower cost.

If the price of movies goes up too high, people may rent home videos. The level of demand for movies goes down while the level of demand for home videos goes up.

People who buy bicycles for recreation have many substitute products to choose from. Some of these substitute products cost less than bicycles.

On the other hand, people who buy bicycles for transportation may not have any good substitute product within the same price range. Automobiles and motorcycles are both more costly.

How Much Satisfaction People Get From the Product

In general, people spend their money on what gives them pleasure or satisfaction. People who really enjoy bicycling or who feel it is their best means of transportation may decide to do without something else and buy a new bicycle even if prices are high. Less enthusiastic bicyclists are likely to choose a substitute product.

The Size of the Market for a Particular Product

> ❖ **Market size** = The number of potential customers for a particular product

In general, the level of demand will be larger for a product with a large market size than for a product with a small market size because a product with a large market size has more potential customers.

The level of demand for $2,000 custom-made racing bikes in Barnsville is far less than the level of demand for *Sprints*. Few people in Barnsville need or want expensive racing bikes.

Because of the smaller market, you can never hope to sell very many custom-made racing bikes in Barnsville, even if you drop the price as low as possible. Racing bikes just don't do the job that the people in Barnsville want.

2. THE DEMAND FOR CONSTRUCTION WORKERS IN JONESVILLE

The kind of demand you have been reading about so far in this chapter is called consumer demand. But demand exists for workers and employees, too.

Several builders and construction companies in the town of Jonesville need employees. Figure 5–6 shows how many workers all the builders are willing to hire at different wages.

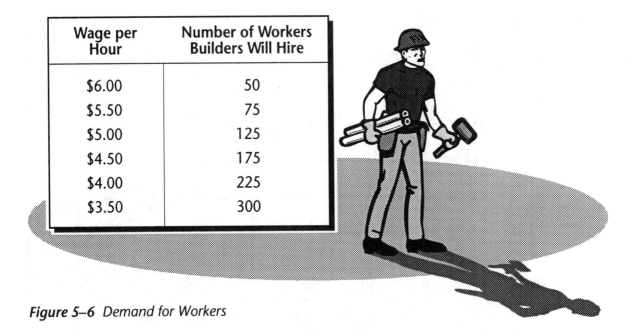

Wage per Hour	Number of Workers Builders Will Hire
$6.00	50
$5.50	75
$5.00	125
$4.50	175
$4.00	225
$3.50	300

Figure 5–6 *Demand for Workers*

The left-hand column of Figure 5–6 shows six different possible wages for building and construction workers in Jonesville. The highest wage ($6.00) is at the top of the column. As you read down this column, the wages get lower. The lowest wage ($3.50) is at the bottom of the column.

The right-hand column of Figure 5–6 shows the number of workers the builders are willing to hire at each of the six wages. The smallest number of workers (50) the builders are willing to hire at any one wage is at the top of the column. As you read down this column, the numbers get larger.

The largest number of workers (300) the builders are willing to hire is at the bottom of the column.

Notice that as the wage drops, the number of workers that builders are willing to hire gets larger and larger.

Figure 5–6 says that all together, the builders in Jonesville are willing to hire 300 workers at $3.50 an hour. As wages go up, however, the builders are willing to hire fewer workers. At $6.00 an hour, the builders are willing to hire only 50 workers.

The demand curve in Figure 5–7 is a picture of the numbers in Figure 5–6.

The horizontal lines on the graph in Figure 5–7 represent the different hourly wages that building and construction workers might be paid. Six different wages, ranging from $3.50 to $6.00, are printed on the left side of the graph. The highest wage ($6.00) is at the top.

The vertical lines on the graph show how many workers the building and construction companies are willing to hire at each wage. Six numbers are printed at the bottom of the graph. The lowest number (50) of workers demanded at any of these wages is at the left.

Each dot on the graph shows the number of workers demanded at one particular wage. Dot A shows that builders will hire 50 workers at $6.00 an hour. Dot C shows that they will hire 125 workers at $5.00 an hour. Dot D shows that they will hire 175 workers at $4.50 an hour.

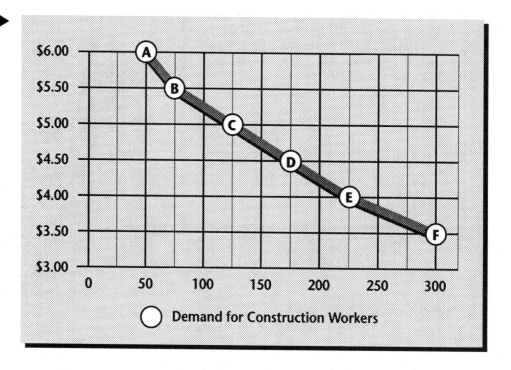

Figure 5–7 ▶
Demand curve for construction workers

• *What does **Dot E** show?*
(Answer: At $4.00 an hour, builders will hire 225 workers.)

Notice that the demand for building and construction workers in Jonesville is an elastic demand. The number of workers demanded by employers changes according to the amount of wages they have to pay.

Think About It

1. State the law of demand.
2. Name two factors that influence the level of demand.
3. Name a product that your family buys whose demand is elastic. Why is demand for this product elastic?
4. Name a product that your family buys whose demand is not elastic. Why is there little change in the demand for this product?

End of Chapter Quiz

Answer True (T) or False (F):

_____ 1. In economics, *demand* means the amount of goods or services people are willing to buy at a given price.

_____ 2. The *law of demand* says that people will buy more of a product at a high price than they will at a low price.

_____ 3. If the demand for a product is *elastic*, the amount demanded will change if there is a small change in price.

_____ 4. Competition from a similar product helps make the price of the product more elastic.

_____ 5. A *flat demand curve* shows that the demand for a product is very elastic.

_____ 6. The demand for luxuries is more elastic than the demand for necessities.

_____ 7. The demand for low-priced items is usually more elastic than the demand for high-priced items.

_____ 8. The level of demand for a product is only influenced by how necessary the product is for people's lives.

_____ 9. When people expect their incomes to go up in the future, the demand for non-essential products often increases.

_____ 10. The demand for a product may go down if a substitute product costs less.

_____ 11. People will often spend money on a product they really like even if the price goes up.

_____ 12. A major reason businesses spend large sums of money on advertising is to make people want their products and thus increase the demand for their products.

_____ 13. *Market size* means the number of businesses selling a certain product.

_____ 14. The demand for laundry soap is more elastic than the demand for new cars.

_____ 15. If the demand for workers in a certain industry is elastic, the number hired will go up as wages go down.

CHAPTER 6

SUPPLY IN A MARKET ECONOMY

What Is Supply?

Producers of goods—shoes or apples or TVs—are willing to sell (supply) products to consumers for a certain price. The price must be great enough for the producer to earn a **profit.**

> ❖ **Profit** = The total amount received from the sale of products minus the cost of producing those products

The greater the profit, the more most producers are willing to produce.

Workers are willing to sell (**supply**) services and labor to an employer for a certain wage. In general, more people will be willing to work as wages go up.

> ❖ **Supply** = the amount of goods or services people are willing to provide at a given price

The Law of Supply

The **law of supply** says that producers will supply more goods and services when they can sell them at a higher price. Producers will supply fewer goods and services when the price goes down.

1. THE SUPPLY OF IDEAL COMPANY'S TELEPHONES

The Ideal Appliance Company makes special-purpose telephones. The number of telephones that Ideal is willing to make depends on the price they can get for each one. Like most businesses, Ideal's goal is to make a profit.

Profits are income for producers. Some producers use part of their profits to expand their business so that they can produce more goods.

In order to make a profit, producers must—

- Produce a product that people want to buy
- Keep production costs low
- Sell the product at a price that people can afford and are willing to pay

Finding A Market

No matter how wonderful a product is, if no one will buy it the producer can't make a profit. Producers must have a market for their products.

Many businesses do market research to find out what products people want to buy. The vast number of ads you see every day are designed to create markets by convincing people that they want to buy certain products.

The Economy Telephone With All the Big Luxury Features!

Now you can have a telephone at home with all the power and features of an expensive office telephone network, for peanuts! The speed and convenience of Automatic Speed Dialing, Re-Dialing, Programmable "Hot" Numbers for frequently-called numbers, ten number buttons, 25' cord, Co-processor Answering Machine (no tape), Call Screening, and many other extraordinary features. See the amazing new **VX-300** Telephone System from The **IDEAL** Telephone Company at your local telephone outlet store, or call us today at **1 – 800 – PHONE – US**

Ergonomic Handset · *Product Name*
IDEAL VX-300
24-Number Speed Dial Memory
Speaker
Ring/Pulse/Message Volume Controls
Power Adapter
Programmable Buttons
Answering Machine Chip and Mike
Special Control Options
25' Cord

Production Costs

Profit is only a part of the price producers receive for their goods. Part of the sale price must pay for **production costs.**

❖ *Production costs = The cost of resources and other expenses related to producing goods*

Low production costs mean that a larger part of the sale price for a product will be profit. Low production costs also help keep the price of goods low and thus increase sales.

The total cost of production includes two kinds of costs:

- Fixed costs
- Variable costs

Fixed Costs

Fixed costs are those costs producers must pay just to stay in business. Fixed costs include:

- Rent
- Insurance
- Machinery and equipment
- Salaries of executives or managers

Fixed costs are the same no matter how much or how little is produced. If a business produces nothing, it still has to pay these costs. Its total costs equal these fixed costs.

Variable Costs

Variable costs are those which change depending on how much or how little is produced.

Variable costs include:

- Cost of raw materials
- Wages for workers

The cost of raw materials and labor will be greater to produce 30,000 telephones than to produce 1,000 telephones because a manufacturer will need more raw materials and more workers to produce the larger number of phones. The more a business produces, the greater the variable costs as well as the total production costs will be.

How Many Telephones Will the Ideal Company Supply?

The Ideal Company figured out the fixed costs and the variable costs for producing different models of telephones. The total costs for producing a model called the VX-300 came to $80.

Ideal decides to sell its Model VX-300 phones for $140 each. It expects to sell 25,000 of this model each year at this price.

If the VX-300 turns out to be a great success, customers may be willing to pay more to get them—for example, $160 or even more. Ideal will raise its prices. At this price it will be making more profit, so it will also make more VX-300s. Or other companies may decide to make models like the VX-300. The supply of VX-300s or models like them will go up.

If, on the other hand, the VX-300 does not do well, or if there are other similar models selling for less money, Ideal will have to drop its prices. It will not make as much money from this model, so it will also make fewer of them. The supply of VX-300s will go down.

Ideal won't supply any VX-300s for $80 or less. It wouldn't make any profit. The supply of VX-300s will drop to zero.

Figure 6–1 shows how many VX-300 telephones Ideal will supply at several different prices.

The left-hand column of Figure 6–1 lists seven possible prices for the Model VX-300 telephone. The lowest price ($100) is at the top. As you read down the column, the prices get larger.

The right-hand column of Figure 6–1 lists the number of VX-300s Ideal is willing to supply at each price. As you read down the column, the numbers get larger.

Price per Phone	Supply of Phones
$80	0
$100	5,000
$120	15,000
$140	25,000
$160	50,000
$180	80,000
$200	150,000

Figure 6–1 Supply of VX-300 Telephones

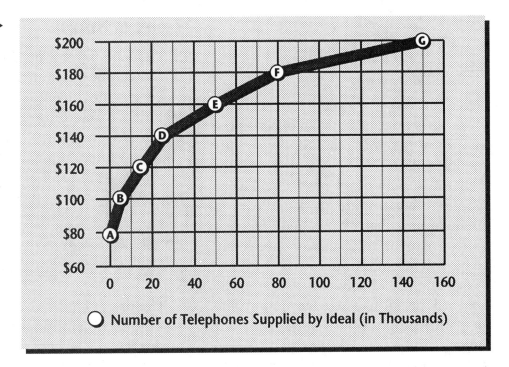

Figure 6–2 ▶
Supply curve for Model VX-300 Telephones

Notice that as the prices get larger, the number of *VX-300s* Ideal is willing to supply also gets larger.

At the low price of $100 for each *VX-300*, Ideal's profit will be very small. Figure 6–1 shows that at $100 each, Ideal is willing to supply only 5,000 of this model. If Ideal can sell their *VX-300* phones for the high price of $200 each, they are willing to supply 150,000 phones.

The graph in Figure 6–2 is a picture of the numbers in Figure 6–1. The line is called a **supply curve.**

The supply curve in Figure 6–2 shows the relationship between the cost of each *VX-300* phone and the number of phones Ideal is willing to supply.

The horizontal lines on the graph represent the possible prices for *VX-300s*. Seven different prices are printed on the left side of the graph. The highest price ($200) is at the top.

The vertical lines on the graph show the different number of *VX-300* phones Ideal is willing to produce. Nine different numbers are printed at the bottom of the graph. The smallest number (zero) is at the left.

Each dot on the graph shows the number of telephones Ideal is willing to supply at a given price. Dot D shows that at $140 Ideal will supply 25,000 *VX-300s*.

- *What does Dot F show?*
  (Answer: At $180, Ideal is willing to supply 80,000 *VX-300s*.)

Changes in Number of Items Supplied Based on Price

Notice that Ideal is willing to supply many more of its special phones every time the price increases by $10. Price makes a big difference in the supply of phones. This is an example of what is called **elastic supply.**

> ❖ **Elastic supply** = Supply that shows a major change as a result of a small price change

Because price has a major effect on the supply of *VX-300*s, the supply of this model is elastic.

Is the supply of all products elastic? No. But items that are quick and easy to produce and that do not require great skill or expensive machinery are likely to have an elastic supply.

The supply of souvenir objects to be sold at a special event is even more elastic than the supply of *VX-300*s. Souvenir items can be produced quickly and easily. When demand and price go up, it is easy for producers to increase the supply of souvenir items.

It is difficult to quickly increase the supply of products that require great skill, expensive machinery, or a long time to produce. A small price change is not enough to change their supply. Therefore, these products do not have an elastic supply.

Apples are an example of inelastic supply. Apple trees take many years to bear fruit. No matter how much the price of apples increased, a grower cannot quickly increase the supply of apples. The supply of apples will not show a major change as a result of a small price change.

Level of Supply

The amount of a product that is produced may be different at different times.

Before the invention of the sewing machine, all clothing had to be made by hand. No matter how much clothing people wanted, the amount of clothing produced—the **level of supply** of clothing—was limited.

> ❖ **Level of supply** = the total amount of a product produced at any one time

The use of high-speed electric sewing machines in clothing factories today means that the level of supply of clothing can be far greater than if clothing still had to be made by hand.

Many factors influence the level of supply of a product. When the level of supply changes, more than one factor may be at work. Some of the factors that influence the level of supply are:

- The cost of production
- New producers in the market
- Changes in technology
- The price of other products

Any of these factors, alone or in combination with each other, may cause the overall level of supply to go up or down.

Changes in the Cost of Production

Increases or decreases in the cost of labor or raw materials influence the level of supply.

A drop in the cost of cotton means that suppliers can now produce more cotton clothing without increasing the cost of their raw materials.

New Producers in the Market

Supply usually increases when new suppliers enter a market. Supply usually drops when suppliers leave a market.

If the number of clothing manufacturers increases, the supply of clothing on the market will probably increase. Later, if one or more of these manufacturers goes out of business, the supply of clothing will probably drop.

Changes in Technology

New technologies may lower production costs, making it easier to produce more goods for sale at a lower price. New technologies may also cause one product to replace another product.

Development of assembly-line production made it possible to produce cars more quickly and easily. As a result the supply of cars increased rapidly. Because of this new technology, however, the supply of horse-drawn carriages dropped rapidly.

More recently, advances in technology have been responsible for rapid growth in the supply of home videos and personal computers.

The Price of Substitute Products

A drop in the price of a substitute product may cause suppliers to cut back on their own production. If the price of cotton clothing goes down, producers may reduce the supply of clothing made of synthetic fibers. They feel that more people will be buying cotton clothing and fewer people will buy synthetic.

Or, if the price of cotton clothing increases, suppliers may produce more clothing made of synthetic fibers.

2. THE SUPPLY OF CONSTRUCTION WORKERS IN JONESVILLE

Now let's look at another kind of supply—the supply of workers in an industry.

In Chapter 5 you read that builders in Jonesville need employees. Now we will look at the supply of labor that construction workers in Jonesville are willing to provide at different wages.

Wages for construction workers in Jonesville range from $3.50 to $6.00 an hour. Figure 6–3 shows how many workers were willing to work for each wage.

Wage per Hour	Number of Workers Willing to Work
$3.50	75
$4.00	150
$4.50	175
$5.00	225
$5.50	275
$6.00	300

Figure 6–3 Supply of workers

The left-hand column in Figure 6–3 shows six different hourly wages. The lowest wage ($3.50) is at the top. As you read down the column, the wages get larger.

The right-hand column in Figure 6–3 shows how many construction workers are willing to work for each wage. Notice that as the wages get higher, the number of workers willing to work gets larger.

The builders in Jonesville found only 75 workers who would work for $3.50 an

Figure 6–4 ▶

Supply curve for workers

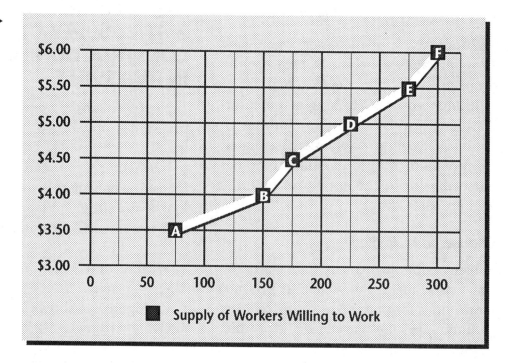

hour. As wages went up, more workers were willing to work. At $6.00 an hour, 300 workers would work.

The supply curve in Figure 6–4 is a picture of the numbers in Figure 6–3.

The supply curve in Figure 6–4 shows the relationship between wages and the number of workers willing to work.

- Horizontal lines on the graph represent possible hourly wages. Six different wages are printed on the left side of the graph. The highest wage ($6.00) is at the top.
- Vertical lines on the graph show the different number of workers willing to work. Eleven different numbers are printed at the bottom of the graph. The highest number (300) is at the right.

Each square on the graph shows the number of workers willing to work at a given wage. Square B shows that at $4.00 an hour, 150 workers will work.

- *What does Square C show?* (Answer: At $4.50 an hour, 175 workers will work.)

Think About It

1. State the law of supply.
2. What is profit?
3. What are fixed costs?
4. What are variable costs?
5. Name two factors that influence the level of supply.

End of Chapter Quiz

Answer True (T) or False (F):

_____ 1. In economics, *supply* means the amount of goods or services people are willing to buy at a given price.

_____ 2. *Profit* is the total selling price of goods or services.

_____ 3. The *law of supply* says that producers will supply more goods and services when they can sell them at a higher price.

_____ 4. Finding a *market* for a product means finding people who are willing to buy the product.

_____ 5. One reason producers want to keep production costs low is to make profits high.

_____ 6. The production costs for most goods are *fixed*. There is little that the producer can do to change production costs.

_____ 7. In general, a company is willing to sell more of a product at a high price than at a low price.

_____ 8. *Elastic supply* means that the number of an item supplied changes when the price of the item changes.

_____ 9. Changes in the costs of production may change the cost of a product but do not affect its level of supply.

_____ 10. The level of supply for most products is different at different times and in different places.

_____ 11. Changes in technology are a major cause for changes in the level of supply.

_____ 12. The level of supply of one product may drop when a new product is introduced and people's tastes change.

_____ 13. When word processors were developed, the supply of typewriters began to drop.

_____ 14. More workers are usually willing to work at a job as wages go up.

_____ 15. Employers are usually willing to hire more workers as wages go up.

CHAPTER 7

PRICES IN A MARKET ECONOMY

Different economic groups have different goals. On the one hand, consumers want low prices, and employers want to pay low wages. On the other hand, producers want to sell their goods for high prices and workers want to earn high wages. These groups must work out a compromise.

Consumers and employers must agree to pay high enough prices or wages to get the goods and services they need.

Producers and workers must agree to accept prices and wages low enough so that they can sell their goods or services.

If a good compromise is reached, workers will earn a living, producers will make a profit, and there will be neither a **shortage** nor a **surplus** of goods or services.

> ❖ *Shortage* = Too little of a product or service to meet the demand
>
> ❖ *Surplus* = More of a product or service than is demanded

The laws of supply and demand help producers find the right price for their products.

Finding the Right Price

A manufacturer in Kansas made 1000 skateboards and decided to charge $50 each. Consumers bought only 200 at this high price. This left a *surplus* of 800 skateboards.

A manufacturer in South Carolina made 1000 skateboards and sold them for $10 each. Consumers quickly bought all 1000 and wanted more. The manufacturer could have sold at least 2000 at this low price. The low price created a *shortage* of 1000 skateboards.

A manufacturer in New Jersey made 1000 skateboards and sold them for $20 each. Within a few months, all the skateboards were sold. Everyone who wanted a skateboard got one. At this price, there was no shortage and no surplus. Supply and demand were balanced, or **in equilibrium.** (The word equilibrium means "balance.")

When the price was too high, few people bought skateboards. The manufacturer was left with a surplus of unsold skateboards and didn't make a profit.

When the price was too low, the manufacturer sold a lot of skateboards and made a small profit. However, the shortage of skateboards showed that the demand for skateboards at this price was great. The manufacturer could have sold more skateboards, or he could have sold them for a somewhat higher price and made a bigger profit.

- When supply and demand are balanced, the market is said to be in a state of equilibrium.

BLOSSOM FARMS AND SELLING CARNATIONS

Blossom Farms wants to raise carnations to sell to local flower shops. Before they plant any seeds, however, they must learn if there is a market for carnations. Blossom Farms wants to be sure they can sell enough carnations to make a profit.

Here are some questions to help Blossom Farms find out how many carnations they can sell:

- ***How big is the market?*** How many flower shops are there in the area? If the area has many flower shops, Blossom Farms can probably sell a lot of carnations. In general, the larger the market, the higher the level of demand.
- ***What is the level of competition?*** How many other growers are selling carnations to these same flower shops?
- ***How much money do people in the area have to spend on flowers?*** If the customers in this area have low incomes, the level of demand for flowers will probably be low. If they have high incomes, the level of demand will probably be higher. Flowers are not a necessity. The level of demand for flowers will probably

Figure 7–1 A Flower Market in a Large City

not be high unless customers in the area have fairly high incomes.

- *Do people in this area like carnations?* Or are other flowers more popular? What other things might customers prefer to buy?
- *How much will flower shops pay for carnations?* Will this be more than production costs? What profit can Blossom Farms make?

Mrs. Clark, owner of Blossom Farms, decides to do some market research. This is what she learns:

- There are many flower shops in nearby towns. The market for Blossom Farms' carnations is large.
- There is some competition. Local flower shops have carnations shipped in. But most florists would probably prefer fresh flowers, locally grown, to flowers that are shipped in from outside the local area. Mrs. Clark has something to offer—fresh flowers—that sets her apart from the competition.
- Most people who live nearby have fairly high incomes. They can afford to buy flowers.
- Carnations are one of the most popular flowers.

So far, things are looking good. Mrs. Clark found positive answers to most of the factors that affect demand.

Now Mrs. Clark must decide if Blossom Farms can make a profit selling carnations. How much should Blossom Farms charge for their carnations? Mrs. Clark does some more research to find out how many dozen carnations were bought by florists in her area at different times and at different prices.

The Demand for Carnations and Their Price

First, Mrs. Clark makes a chart of what she finds about the demand for carnations:

Price per Dozen	Number of Dozen Demanded
$10.00	50
$9.00	500
$8.00	1000
$7.00	1500
$6.00	2000
$5.00	2500
$4.00	3000

Figure 7–1 Demand for Carnations

She finds, as she expected, that the demand for carnations was far greater at a low price than it was at a high price. Figure 7–1 shows that as the price per dozen gets smaller (reading down the left-hand column), the number of carnations demanded gets larger (reading down the right-hand column).

—At $4.00 per dozen (bottom of left-hand column) flower shops were willing to buy 3000 dozen carnations (bottom of right-hand column).

—At $10.00 per dozen (top of left-hand column), flower shops were willing to buy only 50 dozen (top of right-hand column).

- *How many dozen carnations would the flower shops buy at $7.00 a dozen?* (Answer: 1500 dozen)

The Supply of Carnations and Their Price

Next, Mrs. Clark makes a chart of what she finds out about the supply of carnations offered by growers like herself:

Price per Dozen	Number of Dozen Offered
$10.00	3000
$9.00	2500
$8.00	2000
$7.00	1500
$6.00	500
$5.00	100
$4.00	50

Figure 7–2 Supply of Carnations

Mrs. Clark found that as the price per dozen gets smaller, the number of carnations that the growers are willing to grow and sell also gets smaller.

- When carnation prices were only $4.00 a dozen (Figure 7–2, bottom of left-hand column), most flower growers turned to growing something more profitable. Only a few suppliers continued to grow carnations. The supply offered dropped to only 50 dozen. (Figure 7–2, bottom of right-hand column).
- At another time, she found that the price of carnations went up to $10.00 a dozen. Soon all the flower growers were growing carnations. At the high prices of $10 a dozen, suppliers were offering 3000 dozen carnations.

The Equilibrium Price of Carnations

Mrs. Clark wants to sell all her carnations for the highest price she can get. But she knows that if she charges too much, she won't sell all her carnations. And she knows that if she charges very little, she will sell them all, but she won't get the best price. She may not even make a profit.

She prepares a graph (shown in Figure 7–3 on the next page) that combines information from the demand chart and the supply chart.

Looking at the chart, Mrs. Clark sees that when carnations are selling for $9.00 per dozen, there is soon a surplus of carnations on the market. Lots of growers rush in to start growing and selling carnations at this price, but it's too high for most people to pay. The price will have to drop before the surplus gets sold.

On the other hand, when carnations sell for $5.00 per dozen, there is soon a shortage of carnations. Lots of customers will want to buy carnations at this low price. But not many growers will want to resupply carnations for so little money, so the supply will drop. The price will have to go up before most growers will be willing to supply more carnations.

The demand curve and the supply curve cross each other at the point called the **equilibrium point.**

❖ **Equilibrium point** = The point where supply and demand are in balance

At this point, all the carnations are sold. The demand is satisfied. The price at which this happens is the equilibrium price—$7.00.

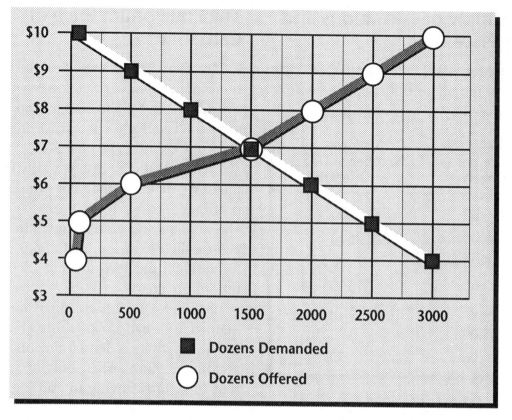

Figure 7–3 Equilibrium Price for Carnations. As prices go up, supply goes up but demand goes down. Supply and Demand balance at $7.00.

Mrs. Clark decides that at a price of $7.00 per dozen she can still make a profit. She decides to go into business selling carnations.

Other Influences on Carnation Prices

Supply and demand are not the only influences on price. For example, Blossom Farms is the only carnation grower in its area. The carnations it sells to local flower shops are fresh. This gives the flower shops a reason to buy from Mrs. Clark that has nothing to do with price. The non-price factor of location gives Blossom Farms an advantage. And so Mrs. Clark may even be able to raise her prices a little. But she can't raise them too much. If she does, the flower shops will go back to buying the cheaper flowers from out-of-town growers.

Think About It

1. What is meant by *shortage?*
2. What is meant by *surplus?*
3. What is meant by an *equilibrium price?*
4. How did Mrs. Clark decide on the price to charge for Blossom Farms' carnations?
5. What might happen to Blossom Farms' business if other growers opened businesses nearby?

End of Chapter Quiz

Answer True (T) or False (F):

_____ 1. The goals of all economic groups in a society are usually the same.

_____ 2. A *shortage* means there is too little of a product to meet the demand.

_____ 3. A *surplus* means that suppliers cannot keep up with the demand for a product.

_____ 4. When a market is in *equilibrium*, there is neither a shortage nor a surplus.

_____ 5. A *surplus* may exist when the price of a product is too high.

_____ 6. When there is a *shortage* of a product, suppliers may be able to sell the product for a higher price.

_____ 7. When Mrs. Clark of Blossom Farms did research on how many customers she was likely to have, she was trying to determine *market size.*

_____ 8. When Mrs. Clark did research on how much flower shops would pay for her carnations, she was trying to find out if she would have any competition.

_____ 9. When Mrs. Clark did research on how many other growers were producing carnations, she was trying to determine production costs.

_____ 10. Mrs. Clark found that flower shops were willing to buy more carnations at a low cost than at a high cost.

_____ 11. Mrs. Clark found that other growers were willing to produce more carnations for sale at a low cost than at a high cost.

_____ 12. The *equilibrium price* for carnations is the price at which the supply and the demand meet.

_____ 13. At the equilibrium price, Mrs. Clark cannot sell enough carnations to make a profit.

_____ 14. Mrs. Clark found that many customers were willing to buy her carnations at a slightly higher price because her flowers were fresh and of very good quality. This is an example of a *non-price factor.*

_____ 15. If other growers began producing carnations in Mrs. Clark's area, the competition would probably drive prices up.

CHAPTER 8

EARNING MONEY IN A MARKET ECONOMY

How much money will workers get for their work?

Wages are the amount of pay a worker earns for a certain amount of work.

- Many workers are paid *by the hour*. A worker who works 40 hours one week will be paid for 40 hours. The same worker may work only 20 hours the next week and will be paid for only 20 hours.
- Some workers are paid *by the piece*, such as how many shirts they sew or how many bushels of apples they pick. These workers are paid only for what they produce. An apple picker may pick 100 bushels one week and 50 bushels the next week. This worker is paid for the 100 bushels the first week but for only 50 bushels the next week.
- Other workers are paid a *salary*, which is a fixed amount of money paid each month.

Wages are **income** for the worker. For the employer, wages are a **cost** of doing business. When wages are spent, they create the demand for consumer goods. If employers did not pay wages, not many people could buy their products and services.

Workers want wages to be as high as possible. Employers want to keep the cost of doing business (including wages) as low as possible. Of course, if all employers succeeded in keeping wages very low, this would cause a problem for employers because the demand for consumer goods would drop. On the other hand, if wages rise too high, the cost of producing goods would rise and their prices would rise too.

AMY STARTS A BUSINESS

Amy is very good at drawing. She has clever ideas about advertising and would like a job designing ads for businesses. She would like to earn $10.00 per hour.

Amy learns that there are very few ad writers in her town. She has seen the ads in her town's newspaper. Most aren't very good. Amy knows she could design better ads.

Since the number of good ad writers in Amy's town is low, Amy believes that she will have no trouble getting a job. She feels sure there is a *demand* for a good ad writer.

Amy makes some sample drawings and visits several businesses.

First Visit: Pizza cafe

Owner: "Your ads are clever, but we already have an ad we run in the newspaper. We've used it for the past five years. It works pretty well. A lot of people eat here. I don't think we need to hire anyone to design new ads for us."

Second Visit: TV repair shop

Owner: "Your ads are good. I painted 'TV repair' and our phone number on some signs and put them on telephone poles around town. Your ads are sure better than that. I'd like to hire you, but I can't afford it. Sorry."

Third Visit: Flower shop

Manager: "These ads are good. Our shop could really use something like this. Most of our customers come in because they see flowers in the window. Some see our name in the phone book. I've beentelling the owner we'd sell more flowers if we advertised in the newspaper. He knows I'm right. And he could afford it. But he doesn't want to spend money on ads."

What a day. The pizza cafe owner didn't want to hire Amy. The TV repair shop wasn't able to hire her. The flower shop wasn't willing to hire her. Pretty discouraging. Everyone likes Amy's ads. No one else in town is drawing ads as good as hers. There should be a demand for Amy's work. But she hasn't found a job.

What's going on?

Buying a Skill

No matter how much need Amy thinks there is for her work, that need doesn't become **demand** unless there is *desire* for it plus *willingness* and *ability to pay for it.*

Fourth Visit: Gift shop

Owner: "Hey, These are good ads. I've been thinking we should do some advertising. It would bring in more business. Yes, I'll hire you. Now, let's talk about pay."

Amy's first success! She has finally found a job.

Amy was right. There is a demand for a good ad writer in her town. Someone *wants* her services, is *able to pay* for her services, and is *willing to pay* for her services.

Amy visits a total of 30 businesses. Twenty of them are interested in hiring her to design their ads. But Amy finds that not all are willing to pay her as much as she wants.

If Amy charges $8.00 per hour, all 20 businesses will hire her. At $8.50 per hour, 13 will hire her. At a wage of $9.00 per hour, only 7 will hire Amy. And at $10.00 per hour, Amy will have only 3 customers.

Figure 8–1, on the next page, shows how many customers Amy will have at different rates per hour.

So what did Amy learn about the demand for ad writers in her town?

The demand for labor is greater at a low wage than at a high wage.

Wages per Hour	Number of Customers
$8.00	20
$8.50	13
$9.00	7
$10.00	3

Figure 8–1 Jobs for Amy

Think About It

1. If you were Amy, what wage would you ask for?
2. Suppose it takes Amy four hours to write an ad for each business. If all 20 businesses hire her, she would have 80 hours of work. How much would she earn if she worked 80 hours at $8.00 per hour?
3. How much would Amy earn if she worked four hours for each of 13 businesses at $8.50 per hour?
4. How much would Amy earn if she worked four hours for each of 7 businesses at $9.00 per hour?

2. WAGES, SUPPLY, AND DEMAND

Wages for Construction Workers in Jonesville

In Chapters 5 and 6 you read about the demand for building and construction workers and the supply of building and construction workers in Jonesville.

The two charts showing the demand for construction workers and the supply of construction workers are reprinted below.

Builders in Jonesville found that the labor supply increased as wages went up (Figure 8–2). More workers were available at $6.00 an hour than at $3.50 an hour.

Workers in Jonesville found that the demand for their labor went up as wages went down (Figure 8–3). Workers who were willing to supply their labor for $3.50 per hour were likely to find jobs more easily than workers who were only willing to supply their labor for $6.00 per hour.

Wages per Hour	Number of Workers Willing to Work
$3.50	75
$4.00	150
$4.50	175
$5.00	225
$5.50	275
$6.00	300

Figure 8–2 Supply of Workers

Wages per Hour	Number of Workers Builders Will Hire
$6.00	50
$5.50	75
$5.00	125
$4.50	175
$4.00	225
$3.50	300

Figure 8–3 Demand for Workers

So what will the workers get paid?

- Builders will choose the lowest wage at which they can get the number of workers they need.
- Workers will take a job at the best wage they can find.

If the builders offer $6.00 per hour, 300 people will apply. But the builders will hire only 50 people at this high wage. Many of the workers, however, will work for less than $6.00 per hour. If the builders can get all the workers they need for less, they will be unwilling to pay $6.00.

Suppose the builders decide to offer $3.50 an hour. Only 75 people are willing to work for $3.50 an hour. If the builders want to hire more than 75 workers, they won't be able to get them.

The Market Clearing Wage

If we draw both the supply curve and the demand curve for workers on the same graph, the two lines cross (Figure 8–4, on the next page). The point at which the two lines cross marks the balance between what the employers want and what the workers want. This point is called the **market clearing wage.**

> ❖ *Market Clearing Wage = The wage at which the number of workers willing to work and the number of workers that builders are willing to hire is equal*

The market clearing wage for the building and construction trades in Jonesville is $4.50 per hour, and the number of people who are hired is 175.

What happens to the 125 workers who wanted to work at $6.00? They obviously don't have jobs in the building industry. Either they must accept a lower wage, find work elsewhere, or have no jobs at all.

Other Influences on Wages

Here are some other important factors that influence wages:

- Competition among employers
- Labor specialization
- Workers' education or training
- Limited labor supplies
- Employers' profits and the price an employer can get for the finished product
- The power of workers united in groups (labor unions)
- Government rules

Competition Among Employers

The market clearing wage for workers in any one job will not necessarily be the same in all areas.

Wages will be higher in an area where there are many employers looking for a skill but only a small number of workers with that skill.

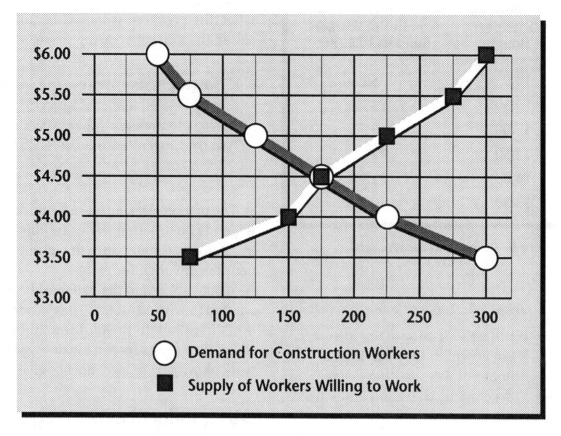

Figure 8–4 *Market Clearing Wage for Construction Workers*

Suppose that Del Rio and Bakersville each have three builders. The market clearing wage for workers in these towns is $4.50 per hour. Then two more builders come to Del Rio. The demand for workers is greater, but the number of workers willing to work for $4.50 per hour is the same. The five builders in Del Rio must now compete for workers. In order to get enough workers, they must raise their wages until they find a new market clearing wage. The change in Del Rio's market clearing wage is not likely to have an effect on Bakersville, however.

Labor Specialization

Workers who have a skill that few other people have may get higher wages. Almost anyone can wash dishes and sweep floors. Fewer people can write ads. Even fewer people have the skills of a doctor. It is not surprising, then, that dishwashers earn low wages, ad writers earn more, and doctors have high incomes.

However, for a specialized skill to bring high wages, it must be in demand. People must want the skill and be willing and able to pay for it. For example, few people today have the skills of stone cutters. Also, few people have the skills of brain surgeons. But the two do not have equal incomes.

Brain surgeons have very high incomes. Stone cutters earn rather low wages. Society places more value on brain surgery than on stone cutting. People today are willing to pay more for brain surgery than for stone cutting.

Education and Training

In general, the more education workers have, the higher the income they can earn. In a recent year, the median family income for families whose head was a high school graduate was almost twice as much as that of families whose head was not a high school graduate.

> ❖ **Median** = Middle point. If you list the income for all families, half of them would be above the median and half of them would be below the median.

The median income for families whose head was a college graduate was more than three times as much as that of families whose head was not a high school graduate.

Limited Labor Supplies

Labor shortages may drive wages up. Because of low pay and often difficult working conditions, the number of people choosing teaching as a career has dropped over the last few decades. Now the shortage of teachers has caused an increase in teacher salaries in some parts of the country.

Limiting the number of workers who can do a certain job also helps to drive wages up. For example, the American Medical Association and medical schools work together to limit the number of people who become doctors.

Employers' Profits

Because wages are part of the cost of doing business, the rate of pay for workers depends on the price employers can get for their products.

Wages are likely to be higher in jobs where employers can get a high price for the finished product. A cook in an expensive restaurant is likely to earn higher wages than a cook in a fast-food restaurant.

Labor Unions

Workers can often get higher wages when they bargain as a group with employers.

You will study about labor unions and the labor movement in Chapter 15.

Government Rules

A federal law sets a **minimum wage** for workers. This law covers about 80 percent of all workers. Today the minimum wage is $4.25 per hour.

The first minimum wage law was passed in 1938 during the Great Depression. At that time, millions of workers were unemployed and wages were very low.

The first minimum wage was $.25 per hour. It applied only to employees of companies that did business across state lines.

Today the minimum wage is seventeen times as much as the first minimum wage. However, because prices are higher now, the actual buying power of today's minimum wage is not even twice as great as the first minimum wage.

Think About It

1. What is meant by the *market clearing wage?*
2. What effect does competition among employers have on wages?
3. What effect does labor specialization have on wages?
4. What effect does education have on a person's income?

End of Chapter Quiz

Answer True (T) or False (F):

_____ 1. The amount of pay a worker gets for a certain amount of work is called *wages*.

_____ 2. A worker who is *paid by the piece* is guaranteed the same fixed amount of pay every week.

_____ 3. Wages are a cost of doing business for employers.

_____ 4. In general, both employers and workers want wages to be as high as possible.

_____ 5. If employers *need* a service offered by an employee, that means there is a *demand* for that service.

_____ 6. As wages go up, the demand for workers usually goes up also.

_____ 7. When many employers want to hire workers with a certain skill, wages will go up.

_____ 8. The more workers there are in an area with a certain skill, the higher wages will be.

_____ 9. The *market clearing wage* is the wage that both employer and employee agree on.

_____ 10. Wages for workers with the same skill are almost always the same in every area of the country.

_____ 11. A skill that is rare and highly valued will earn a higher wage than a skill that almost everyone has.

_____ 12. *Median* means the middle point.

_____ 13. In general, people with a higher level of education earn more than people with less education.

_____ 14. Workers can often get higher wages when they join together in a labor union and bargain as a group with employers.

_____ 15. Every worker in the United States is covered by the *minimum wage law*.

MONEY: WHO NEEDS IT?

Before Money: Barter

What is money? What does it do? Why do we need it?

In today's world, very few people can produce for themselves all the things they need and want. In fact, most people must buy almost all the goods and services they use.

Today most goods and services are bought with money. That is, people exchange money for the goods and services they want. But exchanges of goods and services have not always been made with money.

The most primitive kind of exchange is **barter.**

> ❖ *Barter = trading objects or services directly for other objects or services*

For example, a farm family might give a doctor a chicken or a dozen eggs for treating their child. Or you might mow someone's lawn in exchange for a haircut. This is bartering.

Figure 9–1 Bartering is the most primitive kind of exchange.

In a barter system, you have something of value. You want to trade what you have for something of value—either goods or services—which another person has. But a barter system has some major problems. Let's look at an example.

- You are a farmer with a large crop of tomatoes. The crop is valuable. But you have many more tomatoes than you need. Also, a lot of other people in your town also have a large crop of tomatoes.
- You want new shoes, clothing, a bicycle tire, a movie ticket, and several other things. You would like to trade (barter) your tomatoes for the other things that you want.
- The clerk in the bicycle shop only wants two pounds of tomatoes. But the bicycle tire you want is worth more than the value of two pounds of tomatoes.

The shoe maker already traded shoes for tomatoes with two other customers. Now he has all the tomatoes he wants. In fact, everyone in town seems to have all the tomatoes they want.

Your crop of tomatoes is valuable. But soon the tomatoes will spoil. What will you do if you can't find someone to trade with before your crop loses its value?

You have three main problems:

- You can't find anyone who wants what you have to trade and who also has what you want.
- What you have to trade and what you want are not equal in value.
- What you have to trade may lose its value before you can find someone who wants it.

Bartering is not a very convenient way to trade. It takes a lot of time. With barter-

ing, you may find it hard to get exactly what you want. It is usually hard to find someone who has what you want and wants what you have. Economists call this a **double coincidence of wants.**

So what is the answer? *Money!*

Functions of Money

Money has three main functions. Money is a—

- Standard of value
- Medium of exchange
- Store of value

Money as a Standard of Value

Money is a measure of value—sometimes called a **standard of value.**

No matter what you are measuring—distance, weight, or value—a standard measure is important. A standard measure lets people compare things. It also helps people understand each other.

Distance is measured in inches, feet, yards, and miles. Distance is also measured in centimeters, meters, and kilometers. Weight is measured in pounds or grams. In the United States, value is measured in dollars and cents.

Using money as a standard of measuring value gives people a way to compare the value of one product with another. Money makes it easier for people to keep records of what they buy and sell.

Money as a Medium of Exchange

To make trading easier, groups of people may agree to use a certain type of object to represent the value of all goods and services to be traded.

As you have seen, trading is very difficult in a barter system. So groups of people choose something to be traded for all the things they want to acquire. This symbol is known as **money**. In other words, money is a **medium of exchange.**

A dollar bill is only a piece of paper. As a piece of paper, a dollar bill is not worth much. But as a standard or symbol of value, a dollar bill can be exchanged for many things.

Money makes trade easier. In fact, the trade that goes on between cities, states, and nations today would be impossible without the use of money.

Money as a Way to Store Value

Money is a way to store or keep wealth. Your tomato crop is valuable. It is your wealth. But the tomatoes are only valuable when they are fresh. They won't stay fresh very long.

If you store the tomatoes until next year, they will lose their value. Your wealth will be gone.

However, if you exchange your tomatoes for money, you can store the money as long as you want. You can use the money now or later. Money is a way to store the value of your crop.

Characteristics of Money

Most countries today use paper bills and metal coins for money. In the past, however, many different things have been used for money. Cheese, tea, dogs' teeth, fish hooks, feathers, shells, and many other items have been used for money.

What are the characteristics that money must have? Money must be all of the following:

- Durable
- Portable
- Divisible
- Stable
- Hard to counterfeit (duplicate)

Money Must Be Durable

Whatever is used for money must be sturdy enough to last a long time. That is, it must be **durable**. Metal coins are durable. Paper money is fairly durable, and may be replaced easily and cheaply. Tomatoes, on the other hand, are not durable. Tomatoes would not make good money.

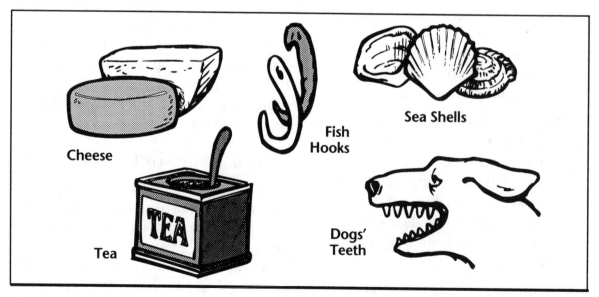

Figure 9–2 All these items have been used in the past as money.

Money Must Be Portable

Whatever is used for money must be easy to carry. It must be convenient for people to use. Small, light-weight coins are easy to carry. Paper money is easy to carry. Tomatoes, of course, would be a real mess to carry around.

Money Must Be Divisible

Whatever is used for money must be easy to divide into smaller units. For example, the dollar is divided into 100 pennies. We call this quality of money **divisibility**. Using money, the value of goods and services can be measured very exactly. It would be rather hard to pay for something that cost half a tomato or a quarter of a tomato.

Money Must Be Stable

Whatever is used for money must keep its value for a long time. It must be something whose supply can be controlled.

If tomatoes were used as money, everyone could begin growing their own. In some years a crop failure could destroy the entire money supply. There would be no way to control the supply of tomatoes. There would be no way to keep the value of a tomato the same for a long time.

Metal coins and paper money are issued by the government. The supply of money is controlled by the government. It is a crime for people to make their own money. Such money, called counterfeit, is worthless. In this way, money is kept scarce. Its value is protected.

It is important to note here the difference between the *face value* of money and the *buying power* of money. Every piece of money has its value printed on it. This is called its **face value.** The face value of money always stays the same.

The **buying power** of money is not always the same. Because of inflation, the buying power of money in the United States has gone down over the last several decades.

> ❖ *Inflation = A rise in the average price level of all goods and services*

You will read more about inflation in Chapter 17. In Chapter 18 you will learn how the federal government controls the supply of money and why the buying power of money is not stable.

Money Must Be Hard to Duplicate

Whatever is used for money must be hard to **counterfeit** or duplicate. Both the material used for making money and the method used for printing paper money or manufacturing coins must be difficult to fake.

What Makes Money Valuable?

To be useful, money must have value. What makes money valuable? Different kinds of money get their value in different ways. The are known as—

- **Commodity money:** The object used for money is valuable in itself.
- **Representative money:** The object used for money stands for something else of value.
- **Fiat money:** The government says the object used for money is valuable.

Commodity Money

The object used for money may be valuable in itself. For example, if diamonds are used as money, then the money is valuable because the diamonds are themselves valuable. An item that has value in itself and that is widely traded is sometimes referred to as a **commodity**, so this kind of money is called **commodity money.**

In the past, many different commodities have been used as money. Some of these are cheese, tea, tobacco, furs, and salt.

Representative Money

The object used for money may stand for something else that has value. Something that stands for something else is said to **represent** it, so this kind of money is called **representative money.**

Checks are representative money. A check can be used in place of cash to buy goods or services. Also, a check can be taken to a bank and exchanged for cash.

In the United States today, checks make up more than 70% of the money supply.

Fiat Money

The object used as money may be valuable because the government says it has value. This kind of money is called **fiat money.** (*Fiat* is a Latin word that means "let it be done." Today, a **fiat** means a government order or decree.) Paper money and coins are fiat money.

A piece of U.S. paper money today is called a Federal Reserve note. Look at a dollar bill. You will see the words, "This note is *legal tender* for all debts, public and private." **Legal tender** means that the bills are recognized by law as money.

Kinds of Money

How many kinds of money are there today? Which of the following are money?

- Paper money
- Coins
- Checks
- Traveler's checks
- Credit cards
- Savings accounts

Cash

Coins and paper money (called **cash** or **currency**) are the most familiar kinds of money today. However, this kind of money makes up less than 1/3 of the total money supply in the United States.

Paper money is now printed in $1, $2, $5, $10, $20, $50, and $100 bills. Coins are made in 1¢, 5¢, 10¢, 25¢, 50¢, and $1 values. Pennies are made from copper and zinc. Other coins are made from copper and nickel. The actual value of the metal in each coin is between 2/10 of a cent and 2 cents.

Remember, paper money and coins are *fiat money.* They have value because the government says they are valuable.

Cash—paper money and coins—serves all the functions of money. Cash can be carried around easily and is a standard of value. Cash is also a way to store value. However, most exchanges that involve money do not use cash. For safety as well as convenience, other forms of money have taken the place of cash in most buying and selling today.

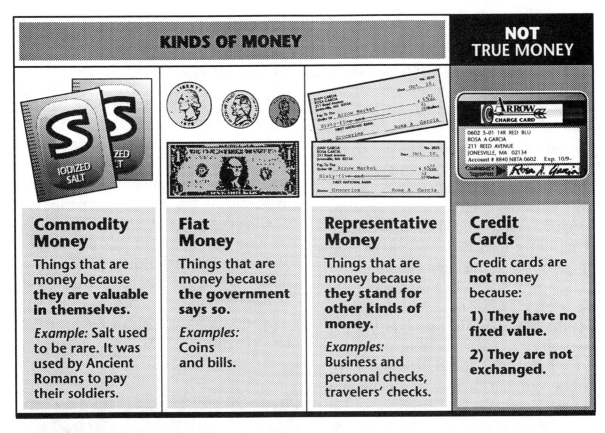

Figure 9–3 *Kinds of Money*

Checks

Checks make up the largest portion of the money supply in the United States today. Remember that checks are *representative money*. Checks represent the money in a checking account.

Checking accounts are also called **demand deposits.** A person who owns a checking account is called a **depositor.** The money in a checking account is available to the depositor at any time. That is, the money is available **on demand.**

Checks are very convenient to use. Checks can be written for the exact amount of a purchase and are accepted by most businesses. Checks are also safer to mail and also to carry around than cash.

Traveler's Checks

Traveler's checks are a special kind of check. They are called checks, but they do not represent money in a person's checking account. They represent money in a bank or a large company like American Express that specializes in these checks.

Traveler's checks are checks that are sold by banks for their face value plus a small fee. They are guaranteed against loss or theft. If a traveler's check is lost or stolen, the bank (or the large company) will replace it. Thus, traveler's checks are safer to carry around than cash.

Traveler's checks are used in place of cash. They are accepted almost everywhere, even in places where the buyer is a stranger. In fact, their name shows that they were invented for use by travelers.

Credit Cards—Are They Money?

Credit cards, sometimes called "plastic," are a common way of buying things. Credit cards are often used instead of cash or checks in buying something. But the credit card itself is not exchanged when you make a purchase with it. And credit cards do not have a fixed value, so they cannot store value. So credit cards cannot really be called money.

Using a credit card means that you are taking out a loan from the credit card company. When you buy something with a credit card, you make a promise to pay later with money. The company that issues the card pays the merchant for the goods you buy. Later, the company sends you a bill listing the things you have bought and the interest the company charges. You make your payment to the credit card company, not to the merchants whose goods you bought.

Savings Accounts

A **savings account** is a way to store value. Also, placing money in a savings account is a way to increase your wealth. Your money earns interest while it is in a savings account.

But a savings account is not a medium of exchange. Money in a savings account cannot be withdrawn by writing a check. It must be withdrawn at the bank. Savings accounts are sometimes called **near money.**

Two kinds of savings accounts are:

- Passbook accounts
- Time deposits

Money in **passbook accounts** may be withdrawn at any time.

Money in **time deposits** is placed there for a fixed period of time—for example, three months, six months, one year, two years, etc. At the end of this period of time, the deposit is said to mature. If you withdraw money from a time deposit before the deposit matures, you must pay a penalty and/or you lose some or all of the interest the money has earned.

Time deposits are also called **certificates of deposit** or **CDs.**

Think About It

1. Give three main problems with bartering.
2. Name the three main functions of money.
3. Why do you think that most countries today use metal coins and paper bills for money?
4. Are checks money? Explain.
5. Why are savings accounts called *near money?*

End of Chapter Quiz

Answer True (T) or False (F):

_____ 1. *Barter* means paying for products with money.

_____ 2. A major problem with the barter system is that the person who has what you want to buy may not want what you have to sell.

_____ 3. Using money as a standard of value gives people a way to compare the value of one product with another.

_____ 4. Money is a symbol of value.

_____ 5. In order for an item to be useful as money, it must be durable.

_____ 6. Gold bricks would make better money than pieces of paper.

_____ 7. Dividing money into small units makes it easy to measure the value of goods very exactly.

_____ 8. Governments control the supply of money so that it will keep its value.

_____ 9. The face *value* of money and its *buying power* are always the same.

_____ 10. *Inflation* means an increase in the value of money.

_____ 11. Printing fake paper money is called *counterfeiting*.

_____ 12. An item such as tea or salt that is used for money is called *representative money*.

_____ 13. The words *legal tender* on dollar bills mean that the bills are recognized by law as money.

_____ 14. Most of the money supply in the United States today is in the form of checks.

_____ 15. Because savings accounts are a way to store value, they are considered as money.

CHAPTER 10

BUSINESS AND INVESTMENT IN A MARKET ECONOMY

1. STARTING A BUSINESS

You Decide To Start a Business

Suppose you want to start a business of your own. You decide to open an art supply shop. You have worked in an art supply store for several years, so you know a lot about art supplies. You are also a good artist. You can sell your own paintings and drawings in your store.

Owning a business yourself would give you a lot of satisfaction. You like to work hard, and you feel sure you can succeed.

You like the idea of being your own boss, making all the decisions about the way to run your business. And since the business will be all yours, the profits will be all yours, also.

- A business owned by one person is called a **sole proprietorship.** The owner is called the **sole proprietor,** or simply the **proprietor.**

Figure 10–1 A Small Business, a Neighborhood Shop

Figure 10–2 *Banks Loan Money to Qualified Borrowers*

You make a list of what you will need to get started:

- a shop
- shop fixtures: display shelves, counter, cash register
- inventory—supplies to sell, in this case, art supplies

Since you plan to run the store yourself, you won't need to hire employees.

Finding Investment Capital

Next, you investigate how much money you'll need to rent a shop and fixtures, pay utilities, and buy your inventory.

You figure it will take about three months before you will be earning enough profit to pay your monthly expenses. You will need **investment capital** of $10,000 to get started and run the business for three months.

> ❖ *Investment Capital* = *Money used to start a business*

You hadn't expected it to be so much. You've been saving for quite some time, but you only have $5,000.

Loans and Collateral

You decide to get a loan. Your credit rating is good, so surely the bank will agree to loan you $5,000.

"I'm starting an art supply business," you explain to the bank loan officer. "I've saved $5,000, but I need to borrow $5,000 more to get started."

"What **collateral** do you have?" the loan officer asks.

> ❖ *Collateral = Something of value that a borrower gives a lender as a guarantee that the loan will be repaid*

79

The only thing you own is your car, but it is old. The bank will loan you only $1,000 on your car.

"This isn't a personal loan," you explain. "It's for my business. I'll be making profits soon. I'm sure I can repay the loan."

"Even for business loans we must have collateral," the loan officer says. "As the sole owner of your business, you are completely **liable** for all the business's debts. A loan to your business is the same as a personal loan as far as the bank is concerned."

> ❖ **Liable** = Legally responsible for something

Other Ways of Raising Investment Capital

"Perhaps a relative might give you a loan," the loan officer suggests. "Or, you could consider getting a business **partner.**

> ❖ **Partnership** = A business owned by two or more people
> ❖ **Partner** = Each owner in a partnership

"Maybe you know someone who would be willing to help finance your business in exchange for a share of your profits."

"I don't know anyone who's interested in running an art supply store," you reply. "Besides, I want to run this business in my own way."

"There are different kinds of partnerships," the loan officer explains. "You can arrange your business any way you want.

"In a **general partnership,** each partner helps finance the business and shares in decision making. Each partner also shares the profits of the business and the liability for all its debts.

"However, you could choose to have a **limited partnership.** A limited partner invests money in the business and shares its profits but has little if any decision-making power. The limited partner is not liable for all the debts of the business. If the business fails, the limited partner will lose only the amount of money invested."

Now you have a choice. You can get a personal loan from a friend or relative, or you can find someone willing to invest in your business in exchange for a share of your profits.

---

2. KINDS OF BUSINESSES

Sole Proprietorships

Seven out of every ten businesses in the United States are sole proprietorships. Almost one-fourth of all business profits are earned by sole proprietorships. However, less than $6 out of every $100 in sales are made by sole proprietorships.

A sole proprietorship is not necessarily run by the owner. In fact, this type of business may have many employees. However, sole proprietorships tend to be small.

Some typical examples of sole proprietorships are—

- Professional offices, such as doctors, dentists, and lawyers
- Services-producing businesses, such as beauticians, laundry and dry cleaning, plumbers, insurance and real-estate brokers, and small construction companies

- Small retail stores, such as grocery stores, florists, and gift shops

The owner of a sole proprietorship has the total responsibility for decision making as well as for the debts of the business. If the business does well, the owner gets all the profits. If the business fails, the owner can lose the business as well as personal possessions to pay off business debts. The failure rate for sole proprietorships is very high.

Partnerships

Only about one in ten of all businesses in the United States are partnerships. Partnerships account for less than $4 out of every $100 in business sales.

Partnerships include many of the same types of businesses as sole proprietorships. Professionals, such as doctors, lawyers, and accountants, frequently form partnerships.

Most partnerships are small businesses that require small amounts of investment capital.

Corporations

Many businesses require larger amounts of investment capital than most sole proprietorships or partnerships have.

In order to get investment capital, a business must have a large number of investors. This is the major reason why businesses **incorporate**, that is, form **corporations**.

- A **corporation** is a business organization that is owned by a group of investors, called its **stockholders**. However, the law treats a corporation as if it were a separate individual.

The biggest businesses in the United States are all corporations.

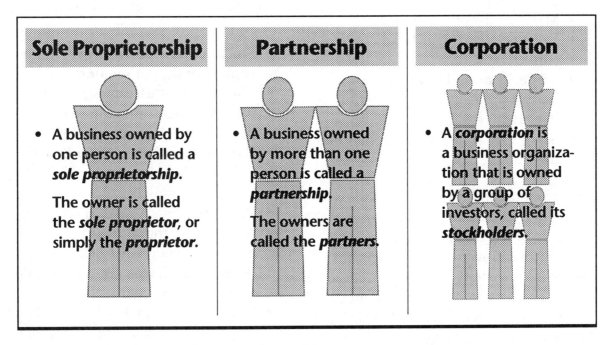

Figure 10–3 Three Types of Business Ownership

3. HOW CORPORATIONS WORK

Incorporating: Beginning a Corporation

A corporation is a much more formal organization than a sole proprietorship or a partnership. People who want to form a corporation must apply for a license, called a **charter**, from their state government. In some states a charter costs a few hundred dollars. In other states, it costs several thousand dollars. The cost of incorporating is one reason many individuals choose to operate their businesses as sole proprietorships or partnerships.

A charter establishes a corporation as a **legal entity.** This means that a corporation is treated as an individual in the eyes of the law.

A corporation can do all of the following things:

- Own property
- Make contracts
- Sell stocks and issue bonds
- Hire workers
- Produce and sell products
- Make a profit
- Pay taxes
- Sue others or be sued in a court of law

A corporation may continue to exist even after its founders die or when its directors or managers change.

About one in every five American businesses is a corporation. However, corporations are responsible for more than $90 out of every $100 in sales in the United States and receive almost three-fourths of all profits.

Who Runs Corporations?

Corporations are run by a **board of directors** chosen by the corporation's owners, or **stockholders**. The board decides—

- What to produce
- How to produce it
- How much to produce
- How to use the corporation's profits
- How much to pay stockholders in dividends

The board also—

- Hires managers and other personnel and appoints a **chief executive officer (CEO).** In many corporations the CEO is also the company president. In other corporations, the CEO and the president are separate officers.

A corporation's CEO is responsible for carrying out the board's policies and running the corporation on a daily basis.

Figure 10–4 is a general picture of how corporations are organized.

- **Stockholders** provide investment capital for the corporation.
- The **board of directors** makes the basic decisions about how the corporation is to operate.
- **Corporate officers**, including the CEO, are in charge of carrying out the board's policies.
- **Vice presidents** head the major divisions within the company. They report to the company CEO.
- **Department heads** are responsible to the vice presidents.
- Each department head supervises **employees** who do the day-to-day work of the company.

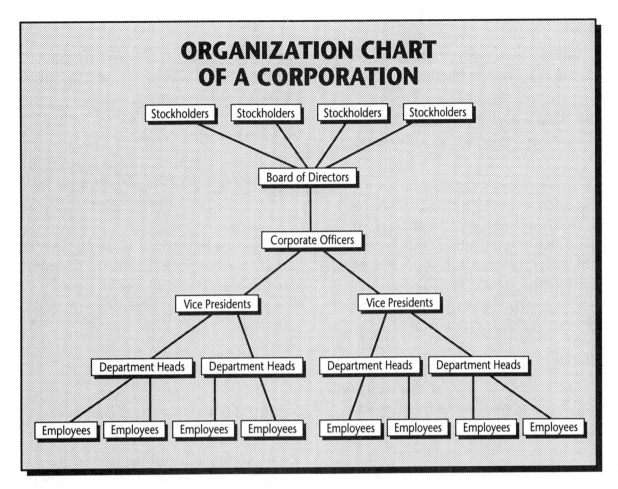

Figure 10–4 *Organization of a Corporation*

Figure 10–5 shows five of the largest corporations in the United States in a recent year and the total sales of each in billions of dollars.

Corporation	Total Sales
General Motors	$125 billion
Exxon	$105 billion
Ford Motor Co.	$98 billion
IBM	$69 billion
General Electric	$58 billion

Figure 10–5 *Corporations with Highest Sales*

Raising Investment Capital for a Corporation

Starting and operating a corporation takes money. This money is called **capital**. Corporations may raise capital from investors by—

- Borrowing money, which the company will then repay to investors with interest. The corporation's promise to repay the loan is called a **bond**.
- Selling shares of ownership in a company. These shares are called **stock.**

Bonds

Corporations can borrow money from investors by selling **bonds.**

> ❖ **Bond** = *A certificate promising to re-pay borrowed money with interest*

Investors buy **corporate bonds** (bonds issued by a corporation) in order to make a profit by earning interest on their investment. Buying a corporate bond does not make the investor an owner of the corporation, however. The bond represents a loan to the corporation, not a purchase of a share of ownership.

Stocks

Corporations also raise capital by selling shares of ownership called **stock**.

> ❖ **Stock** = *Shares of ownership in a corporation*

Investors who buy shares of ownership in a corporation are called **shareholders** or **stockholders**. A corporation is jointly owned by all of its stockholders. Stockholders receive **stock certificates** showing how many shares of the company they own.

Stockholders may sell their shares if they wish. If a corporation goes out of business, the stockholders lose the money they have invested. But they are not personally liable for any of the company's debts.

Stockholders are something like limited partners in a partnership. Even though stockholders own a corporation, they don't have to know anything about running the businesses. They invest to make a profit.

Part of the company's profits are paid to stockholders as **dividends**.

> ❖ **Dividend** = *a share of a company's profits paid to stockholders*

Also, if a business does well, the value of its stock may go up. Stockholders may then sell their shares for a profit.

Corporations sell two different kinds of stocks:

- Common stock, and
- Preferred stock

Stockholders who hold **common stock—**

- Invest money in the company
- Vote for the board of directors who run the corporation
- In some cases, vote on major policies of the corporation
- May receive dividends, although dividends on common stock are not guaranteed

Stockholders who hold **preferred stock—**

- Invest money in the company, just like holders of common stock
- Usually have no voice in running the corporation
- Are guaranteed to receive dividends from the corporation's profits

Think About It

1. Name the three types of business organizations in a market economy.
2. Which type of business organization is the most common?
3. Which type of business organization is responsible for the largest portion of sales?
4. Give one advantage for incorporating a business. Give one disadvantage of incorporating a business.
5. Name two ways that corporations raise investment capital.

4. INVESTING

Suppose you have some extra money that you don't need for day-to-day expenses. You'd like this money to earn a profit for you. Perhaps it's time to learn about investing.

You have heard that stocks and bonds are sold by brokers. So you go to the office of a brokerage firm that you choose from the list of Stock and Bond Brokers in the Yellow Pages.

"I'd like to learn about buying some stocks," you explain to Ms. Ray, one of the brokers. "I have some extra money, and I'd like it to earn as much as it can."

"Well, the stock market might be a good idea for you," Ms. Ray says. "Let me explain how it works."

Buying and Selling Stocks and Bonds

"As you probably know," Ms. Ray tells you, "companies sell stocks and bonds to raise operating capital. We usually call these stocks and bonds **securities**. Brokerage firms like ours sell these securities to investors like yourself.

"There are thousands of corporations that offer stocks and bonds to investors. Most major corporations list their stocks on one of the stock exchanges.

❖ **Stock exchange** = a place where buyers and sellers meet to buy and sell securities

"You've probably heard of the New York Stock Exchange. It's the largest stock exchange in the world. It was started in 1792. It's located on Wall Street in New York City. Then there is the American Stock Exchange. The United States also has 10 regional stock exchanges.

"Brokerage firms must be members of a stock exchange in order to sell the securities listed on that exchange. Our firm is a member of the New York Stock Exchange and also the American Stock Exchange.

"Brokers all over the country trade securities for their customers on these stock exchanges. Sometimes we do business by telephone. Big firms such as ours have computer lines directly to the New York Stock Exchange.

"But we also sell securities that are not listed on any stock exchange. Often new companies or small companies sell securities directly through brokers. We call this the over-the-counter market.

"When you buy securities, you get a receipt that shows the value of the bond

Figure 10–6 The New York Stock Exchange

or how many shares of stock you have bought. This receipt is called a **security.** That's how stocks and bonds came to be called securities."

Bonds

"How would securities earn money for me?" you ask.

"Lets start with bonds," says Ms. Ray. "If you buy bonds, you earn a fixed rate of interest every year for the life of the bond. Then when the bond matures, you get your original investment back plus the last interest payment.

If you buy a five year, $1,000 bond, you'll earn interest for five years and have your $1,000 back at the end of that time."

Stocks

"What about stocks?" you ask.

"Stocks earn money in two different ways," explains Ms. Ray. "They pay dividends, and they may be sold at a higher price than you bought them. Let me explain each way to you."

Dividends

"First, corporations pay **dividends** based on their profits. Most corporations pay dividends four times a year. It's called the quarterly dividend. Others pay dividends once or twice a year. If a corporation is not doing well, it might not pay any dividend at all."

Selling Stock

"But the income from dividends is not the main reason people invest in the stock market. The value of your stocks may go up. If you buy stock today for $20 a share and that stock's value goes up to $25 a share by the time you want to sell it, you've made a profit of $5 for every share of stock that you own. This kind of profit is sometimes called a **capital gain.**

"However, stock prices don't always go up. Sometimes they go down. If the value of your stocks is lower when you are ready to sell than it was when you bought those stocks, you'll take a loss.

"Stock prices go up and down depending on how many shares are for sale and how much investors are willing to pay for the shares. If a corporation is stable and earning a profit, many investors may be interested in buying its stock. We call these stocks **blue chip** stocks.

"If investors lose confidence in a corporation, they may decide to sell the shares they own in that corporation. This can drive the stock's price down."

Speculation

"Some investors specialize in taking chances buying stocks at low prices and selling them when the price goes up. This is called **speculation.** But it is impossible to know for sure exactly when a stock price will go up—or even if it will go up at all. So speculators can lose money as well as make money.

"Stocks don't always earn money for the investor. Sometimes investors lose money. That's why you should never put money into stocks unless you can afford to lose that money," Ms. Ray explains.

Choosing Which Stocks or Bonds to Buy

"How do I choose which company's stocks or bonds I might want to buy?" you ask.

"First of all," Ms. Ray answers, "you should choose a corporation that's in good financial shape. For bonds, look for a good interest rate. You also need to think about how long you want to tie your money up. That means that you need to look at the bond's maturity date. Bonds usually come in large units—$1,000, $5,000, or $10,000. If you have a smaller amount to invest, then bonds might not be for you.

"If you're interested in stocks, it depends on whether you want income or long-term growth of your investment. For income, look for a corporation that's been paying good dividends. For growth of your investment, look for a corporation that has a record of growth. You might also choose one whose stock price is low compared to what it has been recently."

Mutual Funds

"You have another option," Ms. Ray continues. "You could invest in a **mutual fund.**

> ❖ *Mutual fund = a pool of money from investors that is used to buy stocks or bonds*

"A mutual fund is really a special kind of company that buys stock in other companies. It allows many investors to pool their money to invest in a variety of corporations. Some mutual funds invest in bonds; others invest in stocks."

Tax-Free Investments

"If you were in a high income tax bracket, I'd suggest that you might want to consider tax-free investments," Ms. Ray adds. "For example, you don't have to pay income tax on the interest you earn on bonds sold by state and local governments. This kind of bond is called a **municipal bond.** However, the interest rate on municipal bonds is lower than on corporate bonds. So this may or may not be an advantage, depending on what percent of your income you pay in taxes."

The Dow-Jones Industrial Average

"How can I tell how stocks in general are doing?" you ask.

"Have you ever heard of the **Dow Jones Industrial Average?**" Ms. Ray asks you. A lot of people just call it the Dow."

"Yes, I hear how much the Dow goes up or down on the news every night," you tell Ms. Ray. "I always wondered what that meant."

"The Dow is the sum of the closing prices of a selected group of typical stocks. When the Dow goes up, it is a sign that the market is strong. People are buying stocks. Investors have confidence in the market. We call this a **bull market.** When the Dow goes down, it is a sign that fewer people are buying or that stock prices are dropping. We call that a **bear market.**

"How safe are securities?" you ask. "I've heard people talk about stock market crashes and the Great Depression."

"Safety depends on which securities you're talking about," Ms. Ray tells you. "Stock markets crash when investors decide to sell large quantities of stocks, no matter how low the prices go. A crash is the result of loss of confidence in the value of investments. A stock market crash isn't the same thing as a depression. However, the same economic problems that cause a crash can also bring on a depression.

"Government bonds are the safest because they are backed by the government. Some state and local government bonds are also insured. Corporate bonds are safer than stocks. If a corporation fails, it must pay its bondholders before it pays its stockholders.

"Stocks are the biggest risk.

"Well, I'm sure I've told you more than you ever wanted to know about the stock and bond markets," Ms. Ray says. "Here are some data sheets about a few corporations you might be interested in. Give me a call if you decide that buying stocks or bonds is the right investment for you."

Think About It

1. What are *securities*?
2. What is a *stock exchange*?
3. Which stock exchange is the largest in the world?
4. What is meant by *speculation*?
5. What is the difference between *stocks* and *bonds*?
6. Which investments are more risky, stocks or bonds? Why is this true?
7. What is a *mutual fund*?

End of Chapter Quiz

Answer True (T) or False (F):

____ 1. A business owned by one person is called a *corporation*.

____ 2. *Inventory* means the supply of products a store sells.

____ 3. *Investment capital* is the money needed to start a business.

____ 4. When loaning money, the lender usually requires the borrower to have something of value to guarantee that the loan will be repaid.

____ 5. Unlike personal loans, business loans usually do not require *collateral*.

____ 6. In a *general partnership*, all partners are joint owners of the business and are legally responsible for the business's debts.

____ 7. In a *limited partnership*, all partners share equally the decision-making power for the business.

____ 8. Most businesses in the United States today are *sole proprietorships*.

____ 9. *Sole proprietorships* tend to be small.

____ 10. *Sole proprietorships* account for a very high percentage of retail sales in the United States today.

____ 11. Owners of *sole proprietorships* in the U.S. are likely to be successful.

____ 12. Most businesses organized as *partnerships* in the United States are small and require small amounts of investment capital.

____ 13. Businesses offering professional services, such as doctors or lawyers, are common examples of partnerships.

____ 14. Businesses often incorporate to raise more *investment capital.*

____ 15. The owners of a corporation are called the *board of directors.*

____ 16. In the eyes of the law, a corporation is treated as a separate individual.

____ 17. Stockholders in a corporation receive *bonds* showing how many shares of the company they own.

____ 18. A *dividend* is a share of a company's profits paid to stockholders.

____ 19. A *mutual fund* is a company that buys stock in other companies.

____ 20. People who invest in stocks of a *blue-chip company* are guaranteed to make a profit on their investment.

CHAPTER 11

COMPETITION

> ❖ **Competition** = *Rivalry between two or more persons or groups*

In business, **competition** is economic rivalry between producers or sellers of a product.

1. COMPETITION IN THE UNITED STATES

Businesses in the United States have the right to compete with each other to attract customers and sell their goods and services. In fact, the right to compete is protected by law. In many cases, it is illegal for any one producer to control the market for a particular product because this interferes with free competition.

Competition benefits both producers and buyers. For example, competition makes it possible for small producers to participate in the market. Competition also protects consumers by helping to control prices and the quality of goods and services.

Perfect Competition

Perfect competition means that no one buyer or seller is able to control the price of a product. Prices are determined by competition in the marketplace.

Perfect competition exists if—

- Many producers are producing (or selling) the same product or service.
- The products and services made by each producer are exactly the same.
- Each producer is responsible for only a small portion of the total amount of the product offered for sale.
- Many buyers want to buy the product or service.
- All producers and buyers are well informed about the product.
- All producers and buyers are free to make their own independent decisions about prices.
- It is easy for anyone to enter or leave the market—that is, to begin producing the product or service.
- There are no government restrictions or regulations in this market.

Some people believe that perfect competition is the ideal way for markets to operate. They believe that perfect competition is the ideal **market structure.** But perfect competition doesn't exist in the real world.

Small truck farmers (*truck* is a farmer's word for vegetables) who produce vegetables in the United States come the closest to having a purely competitive market.

In the truck-farming industry—

- There are many sellers and many buyers.
- One producer's products are very much the same as those of other producers.
- Usually no one seller controls a large part of the market.
- Producers do not get together to fix the price of their products.
- It is fairly easy for new producers to enter the market.
- There are few government regulations and restrictions.

Still, for most products, perfect competition does not exist.

Monopolies

The opposite of pure competition is a **monopoly**.

> ❖ *Monopoly = Control by one—that is, control of a product or service by one producer or supplier*

In business, a monopoly is a market structure in which one producer (or seller) has total control of the supply and price of a certain product or service.

In a monopoly—

- Only one producer produces a certain product or service.
- The producer controls the price of the product or service.
- No other similar product or service is available for consumers to use as a substitute.
- It is difficult or impossible for other companies to begin producing the product or service.

Even in a monopoly, however, the law of demand influences prices. If prices are too high, consumers will buy (demand) less.

Although in general competition is protected by law in the United States, some types of monopolies are legal. These are:

- Geographic monopolies
- Government monopolies
- Natural monopolies
- Technological monopolies

Geographic Monopolies

A producer or seller may have a **geographic monopoly** simply because no other producer or seller wants to do business in that area. Perhaps a town is too small to support more than one grocery store or gasoline station. Although other producers or sellers are free to enter the market, none has chosen to do so.

Prices are usually higher in small-town stores, partly because there is little competition and partly because these stores buy their inventory in smaller quantities and thus pay higher prices themselves. The law of demand influences prices here, since customers can order items by mail, travel to a larger city to shop, or simply refuse to pay high prices.

In some areas, the development of a large regional shopping center has destroyed the geographic monopoly of small-town stores in the surrounding region.

Because stores in such shopping centers are usually part of larger chains, they can sell for less than small stores. Many smaller stores are driven out of business in this way. The shopping center may then become a geographical monopoly itself.

Government Monopolies

It is sometimes more convenient and practical to allow only one producer to provide a particular product or service.

Products or services that are provided only by governments constitute **government monopolies.** Examples include water and sewer systems, road and bridge building, and postal service. These industries provide for public needs and do not seek to make a profit.

There is no competition in government monopolies. Government officials set prices based on the costs of providing the services.

Natural Monopolies

Sometimes governments give a private company the right to be the sole producer of certain products and services. Examples are gas companies and local public transportation companies. Such arrangements are called **natural monopolies.** Just as in government monopolies, it is more convenient and practical to allow only one producer to provide this particular product or service.

Because there is no competition to help control prices and quality in a natural monopoly, governments make regulations to protect consumers.

Technological Monopolies

Producers who develop new technologies may be given the right to control the production and sale of their new products. This is called a **technological monopoly.** This right is give by the government, just as the right to a natural monopoly is.

New technologies are protected by a **patent.**

> ❖ **Patent** = a document granting the exclusive right to produce and sell a new invention

Writers, musicians, and artists also have the right to a technological monopoly on their work. This right is protected by a **copyright.**

> ❖ **Copyright** = a document granting the exclusive right to publish, duplicate, perform, or sell a written, musical, or artistic work

The right to a technological monopoly encourages people to be creative and develop new products and ideas.

Combinations of Competition and Monopoly

No industry in the United States is a pure competition. Only a few are pure monopolies. Most are a combination of competition and monopoly.

Most industries in the United States today fall into two major categories:

- **Monopolistic competition,** and
- **Oligopoly.**

Monopolistic Competition

Producers often create competition based on something besides price. They may change their products slightly in ways they hope will appeal to consumers. They may also charge a somewhat higher price based on the product's different features. In these ways, producers try to increase both sales and profits.

Labels such as "Taste the difference," "New and improved," "Gets clothes cleaner," "Our brand has more raisins" are designed to convince customers to buy a certain brand. This practice is called **product differentiation.**

> ❖ *Product differentiation = Differences between competing products. The difference may be real or imagined*

Sometimes there is no real difference between two products. Consumers are led to believe there is a difference through advertising. Sometimes the difference is real, but minor.

By creating loyalty among customers to a certain brand name, a producer can charge a higher price for a product, even if the product is virtually the same as another producer's product.

Such non-price competition creates **monopolistic competition.**

Monopolistic competition has some of the same features as pure competition:

- Many producers are producing (or selling) a product or service.
- Each producer is responsible for only a small portion of the total amount of production in the industry.
- Many buyers want to buy the product or service.
- All producers and buyers are well informed about the product.
- All producers and buyers are free to make their own independent decisions about prices.
- It is easy for anyone to enter or leave the market.
- There are few government restrictions or regulations in this market.

However, in monopolistic competition, all products are not exactly the same. Each producer's product or service is different—or consumers believe it is different—from competing products or services.

Producers have more control over the price of their products in a monopolistic competition than in pure competition. However, the law of demand also influences prices. If prices are too high, consumers will buy another product even if they believe it is not quite as good.

Oligopoly

Many industries are dominated by a few large producers. The automobile industry is a good example. This type of market structure is called an **oligopoly**.

> ❖ *Oligopoly = Control by a few—that is, control of a product or service by a few producers or suppliers*

In an oligopoly—

- Only a few producers make a product.
- Each producer is responsible for a large portion of the total amount of production in the industry.
- Each producer has more control over prices because fewer producers are competing.
- It is difficult for new producers to enter the market because start-up costs are high or specialized knowledge is required.

When only a few producers control a particular industry, the actions of any one producer have a powerful effect on prices in the entire industry.

In some oligopolies, each producer sets its prices independently. This practice often results in an unstable market. Each producer is unsure of what the others will do. If one lowers prices, the others may feel that they have to do the same, whether they can afford to or not.

For example, if Ford cuts the price of its cars, General Motors and Chrysler will also either have to cut their prices or lose sales. Such actions can result in a price war. Price wars are good for consumers. However, if prices drop too low and a producer loses too much money, that producer may go out of business.

Sometimes producers in oligopolies have made secret agreements with each other to fix prices at a certain level rather than compete. **Price-fixing**, also called **collusion**, is illegal because it interferes with free competition. Producers who engage in price-fixing can be fined and sent to jail.

Often the smaller producers in an oligopoly will follow the pricing actions of the largest producer. The largest producer then becomes the **price leader**.

Most oligopolies prefer non-price competition. They use the same kinds of non-price competition that monopolistic competitors do. They advertise special features of their products or offer special services in order to attract consumers. In this way, each producer can attract a share of the market without risking the instability of price competition.

Think About It

1. Give three features of *perfect competition*.
2. Give three features of a *monopoly*.
3. What is a *geographic monopoly*?
4. What is a *technological monopoly*?
5. What is meant by *product differentiation*?
6. Compare a pair of low-cost jeans with a pair of designer jeans. What differences do you see in the two pairs? What is the difference in their prices? Are the designer jeans worth the extra money? Why or why not? If you were planning to buy jeans, which pair would you buy?

2. INTERNATIONAL COMPETITION AND INTERNATIONAL TRADE

International Trade

U.S. businesses also have competition from businesses in other countries.

Many goods that are sold in the United States are produced in other countries and **imported** into the United States.

❖ *Import* = To bring something from one country into another country

In addition, many goods that are produced in the United States are **exported** to other countries to be sold there.

❖ **Export** = *To send something from one country to another country*

Importing and exporting between countries of the world is called **international trade.**

Why do nations import and export goods? One reason is that all countries cannot produce the same things. Differences in climate and natural resources influence what a country can produce. Some countries have the natural resources to produce oil. Others can produce coffee. Oranges won't grow in Canada's cold climate. Japan is too mountainous to produce large crops of wheat.

Differences in the size and training of a country's labor force and the level of their technology also influence what can be produced. An industrialized nation such as the United States can produce machinery and consumer goods. Less developed countries must import these things. International trade allows countries to buy things they cannot produce for themselves.

Specialization

International trade creates new markets for a country's goods. This allows producers to concentrate on producing what they do best, that is, to specialize.

❖ **Specializing** = *Producing one kind of goods rather than a variety of goods*

Let's look at an example. Central and South American countries can produce more coffee than the United States. They can also produce coffee at a lower cost than the United States. The climate and soil of Central and South American coun-

tries give them an **absolute advantage** when it comes to growing coffee.

❖ **Absolute advantage** = *A producer can produce more of a product at a lower cost in one country than in another country*

It makes economic sense for countries with such an advantage to specialize in producing coffee. It makes economic sense for them to export coffee and for the United States to import coffee.

Specialization greatly increases productivity. If all producers specialize in what they produce best, total production increases. More goods are available to everyone.

However, the more producers specialize, the less self-sufficient they become. Nations today depend on each other—through international trade—for many of the products they need and want. This is called **economic interdependence.**

In the production of manufactured goods, this kind of specialization is less important. More and more countries are becoming industrialized. They are able to produce the same kinds of products for the international market.

Comparative Advantages

The United States is very rich in resources. Producers in the United States can produce a great many different products. However, producers in the United States still choose to specialize.

How do U.S. producers choose which products to produce? Many producers choose the product that gives them the greatest economic benefits compared with other products they might produce. This is called a **comparative advantage.**

> ❖ *Comparative advantage = A product has a lower alternative cost compared with another product*

Remember that the *alternative cost* is what you give up when you decide to use economic resources in one way instead of another way.

Balance of Trade

> ❖ *Balance of trade = The difference between the value of what a country imports and what it exports*

If a country **imports** (buys from other countries) more than it **exports** (sells to other countries), it has a **trade deficit.** This is sometimes called an **unfavorable balance of trade.**

If, on the other hand, the country exports (sells to other countries) more than it imports (buys from other countries), it has a **trade surplus.** This is also called a **favorable balance of trade.**

Free Trade or Protectionism?

Some products that are imported, such as cars, are also made in the United States. If too many cars are imported, or if imported cars sell for less than U.S.-made cars, U.S. producers will lose money. People will buy imported cars instead of U.S.-made cars.

Some people believe that U.S. producers should be **protected** from foreign competition. Other people believe that **free trade** is the best policy.

Free Trade

Free trade means that each country's businesses are free to export and import what they wish at whatever prices they wish. Free trade increases competition. Free trade can provide lower prices and better quality products.

Supporters emphasize that free trade is good only if it is fair trade. All countries must operate fairly. It is not fair for a country to sell its goods below their cost in order to drive competition out of the market.

One problem with free trade is that wages for workers, a production cost, are much lower in some countries than in other countries. For example, shoes imported from an Asian country can sell for far less than shoes made in the United States. In Asia wages may range from only $.50 to $1.50 an hour. Here, wages are much higher.

Protecting U.S. Producers

Protectionism means that government places certain controls on foreign trade to protect U.S. producers. The two major controls government might use are **import tariffs** and **import quotas.**

> ❖ *Tariff (also called a **Duty**) = A tax on imported goods*

The seller of an imported product has to include the tariff in the cost of the product. The cost of a similar product made in the U.S. would not include this added tariff.

If a high tariff on imported shoes makes them more expensive than U.S.-made shoes, consumers will be more likely to buy U.S.-made shoes.

The other control on imported goods is an import quota.

> ❖ **Import quota** = A limit on how much of a product that can be imported

If Congress passes an import quota for cars, only a certain number of cars can be imported. This protects U.S. car manufacturers by reducing their competition.

Foreign Currency

Most countries have their own **currency** or **money system.**

> ❖ **Currency** = Coins and paper money

Currencies are different in different countries. If you went to Japan you would not buy things with dollars. You would need *yen*.

Figure 11–1, at the top of the next column, gives the unit of measure for currency in several countries.

In general, currencies are bought and sold on the world market. If you plan a trip to Italy, you will need to buy *lira*. To buy things in Italy, you must use *lira*, not dollars.

You may buy *lira* at banks in the United States before you go to Italy. Or, you may buy *lira* at a bank or foreign currency exchange after you get to Italy.

Suppose you have some *lira* left when you are ready to leave Italy. If you plan to visit another country, say France, you can use your extra *lira* to buy *francs*. When you are ready to come home, you can use any *lira* or *francs* you have left to buy dollars.

Country	Currency
Brazil	cruzeiro
Britain	pound
Canada	Canadian dollar
China	yuan
France	franc
Germany	mark
Israel	shekel
Italy	lira
Japan	yen
Mexico	peso
Spain	peseta
U.S.	U.S. dollar

Figure 11–1 Foreign currency

Importers who buy products from a foreign country must pay for the products with the selling country's currency. Products imported from Germany must be paid for with *marks*. Products from China must be bought with *yuan*.

Exchange Rate

The value of the dollar compared with foreign currencies is called the **exchange rate.**

> ❖ **Exchange rate** = the amount of one currency that must be traded to get an equivalent amount of another currency

The exchange rate for the world's currencies is flexible. From day to day the cost of buying a Mexican *peso*, a Japanese *yen*, a British *pound*, or any other foreign currency changes. The price of each currency is set by supply and demand.

The value of foreign currencies compared with the dollar is published in some newspapers in the United States.

Think About It

1. Why does a country *specialize* in a certain product?
2. What are some of the advantages of *economic interdependence?* Can you think of any disadvantages? Explain.
3. What is a *trade deficit?*
4. What is a *trade surplus?*
5. How would a *tariff* protect U.S. producers?
6. What are the advantages of *free trade?*
7. What kind of money would you use to buy things in Mexico?

End of Chapter Quiz

Answer True (T) or False (F):

_____ 1. Competition is protected by law in the United States.

_____ 2. In *perfect competition*, government regulates business activities.

_____ 3. In a *monopoly*, one producer or seller has total control of the supply and price of a certain product.

_____ 4. A *patent* protects an inventor's right to produce and sell a new invention.

_____ 5. A *copyright* is an example of a *technological monopoly*.

_____ 6. Most businesses in the United States today are a combination of competition and monopoly.

_____ 7. Producers can only use advertising based on *product differentiation* when the product they sell is completely different from all other products.

_____ 8. The *law of demand* does not apply in *monopolistic competition*.

_____ 9. In *monopolistic competition*, all producers and buyers are free to make their own decisions about prices.

_____ 10. *Monopolistic competition* can only exist in markets that are dominated by a few large producers.

_____ 11. In *monopolistic competition*, it is very difficult for new producers to enter the market.

_____ 12. *Oligopoly* means control by a large group.

_____ 13. The largest company in an *oligopoly* often becomes the *price leader*.

_____ 14. Most oligopolies prefer competition based on special features of their products rather than competition based on price.

_____ 15. *Price-fixing* encourages competition.

_____ 16. *Price wars* are good for both customers and businesses.

_____ 17. *Exports* are goods brought into one country from another country.

_____ 18. If a country *exports* more than it *imports*, it will have a *favorable balance of trade*.

_____ 19. In *free trade*, businesses selling goods to other countries can set their own prices.

_____ 20. A *tariff* on goods imported from another country is one way of protecting U.S. producers.

INCOME IN THE UNITED STATES

CHAPTER 12

This chapter will look at the income of some different groups in the United States today.

Weekly Earnings

Figure 12–1 is a picture of the **median** weekly earnings of full-time wage and salary workers in the United States.

> *Median* = *middle point. If you list the earnings of all workers in a particular job, half of the workers will make more than the median and half will make less.*

The graph shows the weekly earnings of workers in seven categories. The longer the bar, the larger the earnings for that particular group.

- **White-collar workers** include technicians, salespersons, and office workers.
- **Skilled blue-collar workers** include mechanics, repairers, and construction workers.
- **Semi-skilled blue-collar workers** include truckdrivers, machine operators, factory assemblers, and laborers.

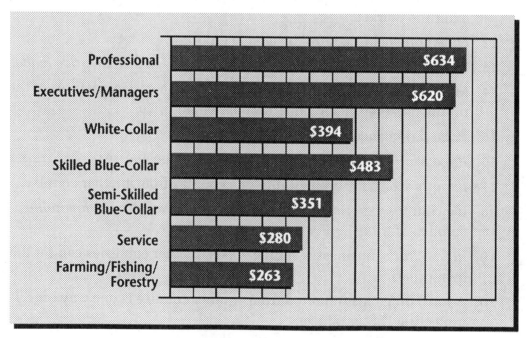

[Source: BLS, *Employment and Earnings*, January 1992, p. 231, 1991 annual averages]

Figure 12–1 *Median Weekly Earnings of Full-Time Wage and Salary Workers*

- **Service workers** include guards, hairdressers, health care aides, and workers in child care, food services, and cleaning services.
- In which job category are earnings the largest?
  (Answer: Professional)
- In which two job categories are earnings the lowest?
  (Answer: Service and Farming/ Fishing/Forestry)
- Who earns more, white collar workers or blue collar workers?
  (Answer: Skilled blue collar workers earn more than white collar workers; semiskilled workers earn less.)

Figure 12–2 shows the average weekly earnings of all workers except supervisors in five different job categories.

Each bar represents the average earnings of workers in one of the five job categories. The dollar amount is printed on that job's bar on the graph.

The average weekly earnings of construction workers ($534) are the highest on the chart. The average weekly earnings of retail sales clerks ($200) are the lowest on the chart.

- Which job category has the second-highest earnings?
  (Answer: Transportation/Utilities)
- If a construction worker works for 50 weeks in a year, how much money does he or she earn in a year?
  (Answer: $26,700)

Figure 12–3, on the next page, shows the median weekly earnings for full-time white, African American, and Latino workers 16 years old and over.

The black bar shows the median earnings of all full-time workers 16 years old and over ($430).

Remember: **Median** = middle point

Note that the median weekly earnings for white workers is above the median for all workers. The median weekly earnings for both African-American and Latino workers is below the median for all workers.

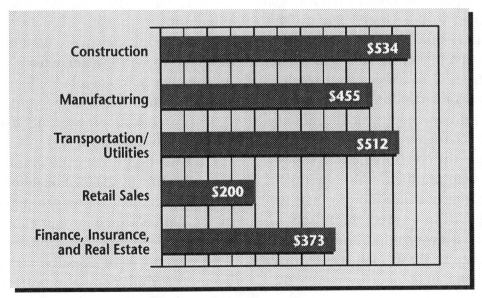

[Source: BLS, *Employment and Earnings,* January 1992, p. 239, 1991 annual averages]

Figure 12–2 Average Weekly Earnings in Five Job Categories

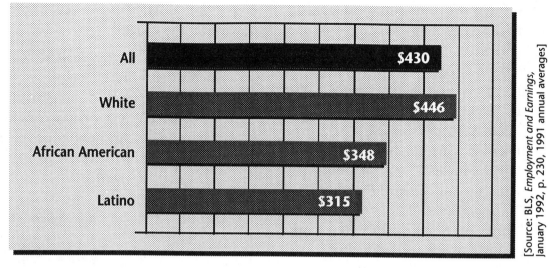

[Source: BLS, *Employment and Earnings*, January 1992, p. 230, 1991 annual averages]

Figure 12–3 Median Weekly Earnings for Full-Time Wage and Salary Workers by Race/Ethnic Group

- Which group had the lowest median weekly earnings?
  (Answer: Latinos)
- What are the median weekly earnings for African-American workers?
  (Answer: $348)

- What is the median income for male high school graduates?
  (Answer: $21,546)
- What is the median income for female high school graduates?
  (Answer: $10,818)

Income and Education

Figure 12–4 shows the relationship between income and education for men and women in the United States. This graph shows that higher education usually means a higher income. This is not always true, of course. School teachers are one major exception to this rule.

Men who are high school graduates have a much higher median income than men who didn't finish high school. Women who are high school graduates have a higher median income than women who didn't finish high school. However, at every education level the median income for women is a lot lower than the median income for men.

Distribution of Income

Income in the United States is not evenly distributed among the whole population.

Some people have very high incomes; others have very low incomes.

The highest 5% of all U.S. households receive 18% of the total U.S. income.

Figure 12–5 shows how income in the United States is distributed.

Each section of the pie graph represents one-fifth of all U.S. households. The size of each slice shows the percentage of the nation's income that each group receives.

If income were equally distributed among the whole population, all the slices of the pie graph would be the same size.

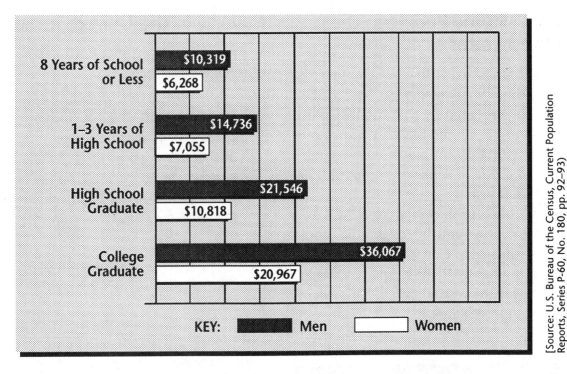

[Source: U.S. Bureau of the Census, Current Population Reports, Series P-60, No. 180, pp. 92–93]

Figure 12–4 Income and Education for Men and Women

Each fifth of all U.S. households would have one-fifth of the nation's total income.

However, the slices are not equal. The slice for the highest-ranking fifth of the population is very large. This group receives almost half (47%) of the nation's total income.

As you go around the graph, each slice gets smaller. This means that each group receives a smaller portion of the nation's total income. The second highest fifth of the population receives 24% of the nation's total income. The lowest fifth of all U.S. households receives only 4%.

- What percentage of the nation's total income does the next-to-lowest fifth of U.S. households receive?

  (Answer: 10%)

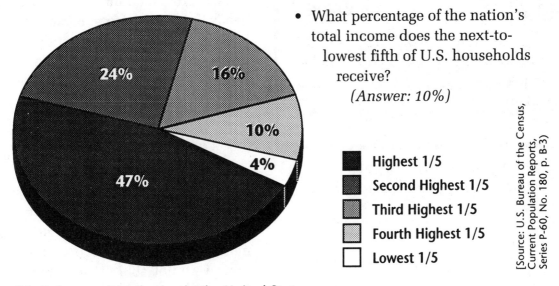

[Source: U.S. Bureau of the Census, Current Population Reports, Series P-60, No. 180, p. B-3]

Figure 12–5 Income Distribution in the United States

High-Income People in the United States

The highest executive in a company is called the Chief Executive Officer (CEO).

CEOs are among the highest-paid people in the United States. Figure 12–6 shows the total earnings of the ten highest paid CEOs in American corporations in a recent year.

The total income of these CEOs includes salaries and bonuses plus stock options and gains. Corporate officers have the option to buy their company's stocks at a lower-than-usual price. This often results in large gains.

Executive Pay

Company	CEO Earnings
Heinz	$75.1 million
Medco Containment	$34.6 million
U.S. Surgical	$23.3 million
Tele-Communications	$18.9 million
National Medical Enterprises	$17.5 million
Toys 'R' Us	$16.4 million
Primerica	$16.1 million
Bristol-Myers Squibb	$12.8 million
Great A&P Tea	$11.0 million
W.R. Grace	$10.0 million

Figure 12–6 Annual Earnings of Ten High-Paid CEOs in United States

Poverty in the United States

Every year government officials set an official poverty line.

> *Official poverty line* = an income based on an "economy" food budget drawn up by the U.S. Department of Agriculture. This budget would allow a family to buy enough food to survive for a short time

A poverty income means that a family cannot buy some of life's basic necessities.

If it buys adequate food, its housing and clothing will not be adequate. If it buys adequate housing, it will not have adequate food.

In a recent year, the official poverty level for one individual living alone was $6,932 (total yearly income). The official poverty line for a family of four—two adults and two children—was $13,812. In this year, almost 36 million Americans were below the official poverty income line. This was more than 14 out of every 100 people in the United States.

The actual amount of income a family needs for a minimum standard of living—that is, to live above a deprivation level—is about twice the official poverty level.

> *Deprivation* = to be unable to get some of life's necessities

The number of people below a deprivation level was more than twice the official poverty count. This means that more than 28 out of every 100 Americans were not able to get some of life's necessities.

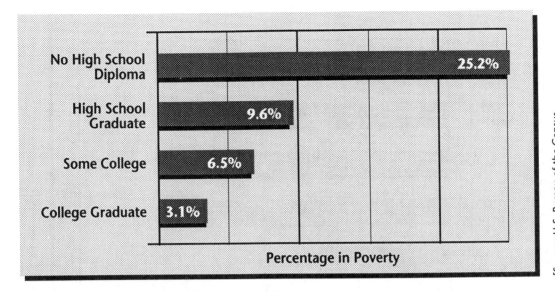

[Source: U.S. Bureau of the Census, Current Population Reports, Series P-60, No. 180, pp. 70-72]

Figure 12–7 Education and Poverty

Education and Poverty

Figure 12–7 shows the relationship between education and poverty at four levels of education: college graduate, some college, high school graduate, and no high school diploma. Each bar shows the percentage of adults 25 years old and older in poverty at that level of education.

Notice that as the level of education goes up, the percent in poverty goes down.

Those who didn't graduate from high school are more than two-and-one-half times as likely to be poor as those who are high school graduates.

- What percent of those who didn't finish high school are poor?
  (Answer: 25.2%)

Poverty and Racial/Ethnic Groups

Two-thirds of all Americans who live in poverty are white. This is partly because whites make up the largest racial/ethnic group in the country. However, people in racial and ethnic minority groups have a greater risk of being in poverty than white people do. That is, the percentage of racial and ethnic minority group members in poverty is higher than the percentage of white people in poverty.

Figure 12–8, on the following page, shows the percent of whites, African Americans, Native Americans, Asian/Pacific Island Americans, and Latinos who were in poverty according to the last census.

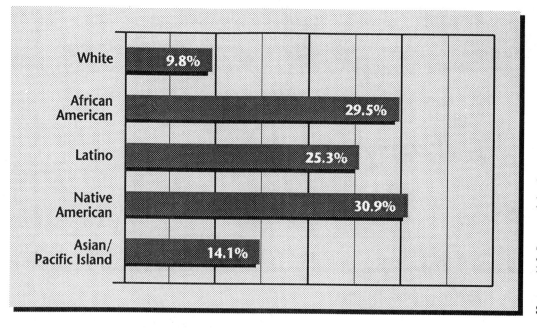

[Source: U.S. Bureau of the Census, *Minority Economic Profiles: 1990.*]

Figure 12–8 *Poverty by Racial/Ethnic Group*

Out of every 100 African Americans, almost 30 are in poverty. Out of every 100 Latinos, just over 25 are in poverty. Out of every 100 whites, 10 are in poverty.

- Which group has the highest poverty rate? What is the poverty rate for this group?
  (Answer: Native Americans; 30.9%)
- What is the percentage of Asian/ Pacific Island Americans in poverty?
  (Answer: 14.1%)

Think About It

1. What is the relation between income and education?
2. Is income in the United States evenly distributed among the whole population?
3. What is meant by the official poverty line?

End of Chapter Quiz

Answer True (T) or False (F):

____ 1. In general, people in professional and managerial jobs earn more than people in construction and factory Jobs.

____ 2. The category of skilled *blue-collar workers* includes mechanics and construction workers.

____ 3. The category of *white-collar workers* includes salespeople and office workers.

____ 4. On the average, Latino-American and African-American families earn about the same as all American families.

____ 5. Education has very little influence on a person's income.

____ 6. In the United States today, income is not evenly distributed among the whole population.

____ 7. In the United States today, the lowest fifth of the population receives about one-fifth of the nation's total income.

____ 8. Some corporate executives in the United States today receive a yearly income of several million dollars.

____ 9. Almost no one in the United States is below the government's official poverty line.

____ 10. In general, a person's chances of living in poverty go down as their level of education goes up.

CHAPTER 13

LABOR IN A MARKET ECONOMY

1. YOU AND THE LABOR MARKET

Why Work?

Why work? There are obviously a lot of other ways to spend your time: sports, dancing, painting, playing music—the list could go on and on.

For most people, the answer to "Why work?" is "I have to! I have to work to earn money."

It costs money to live in today's world. Most food, clothing, housing, and other material things people need are only available for money.

How can you get money? Inherit it? Beg, borrow, or steal?

A few people inherit wealth and don't have to work to survive. Begging usually won't provide enough money for a very comfortable life. Most people can't borrow money unless they have a job. Stealing is illegal and also very risky.

For most people, the only way to get enough money to live is to work.

So, what kind of work do *you* want to do?

The Labor Market

When you start looking for work, you are in the **labor market.**

"Labor market?" you ask. "I just want a job. I just want to earn money to pay my bills and buy things. What does a labor market have to do with getting a job? What is a labor market, anyway?"

In Chapter 3 you learned that the word *market* refers to the actions of buying and selling. A labor market also involves buyers and sellers.

- The *sellers* are the workers who want to sell their labor.
- The *buyers* are the employers who want to buy that labor.
- The *action* in the labor market is the exchange of labor for money.

Workers in the labor market are called the **work force** or **labor force.** Employers include business and industry.

Why Do Employers Want to Buy Labor?

It is easy to see why workers want to sell their labor. They need money.

But why do employers want to buy labor? Employers also want money. Business and industry get their money from selling products and services. Without labor to produce the goods and perform the services, business and industry would have nothing to sell.

Getting A Job

How do you get into the labor market? How do you get a job?

The first thing you must do is find out what jobs are available. Visit employers, fill out applications, have interviews.

But how do you know if you will really get a job? The answer to this question is more difficult. Not everyone who wants to work can find a job.

Getting a job depends on several things. Three of the most important questions are:

- What do you want?
- What does the employer want?
- What is the condition of the labor market?

What You Want

What do you want from a job? Most people want a good quality job with good pay.

Here is a list of things that most workers want from a job:

- A job they enjoy
- A pleasant working atmosphere
- A clean and safe work place where they are not surrounded by poisons
- Work that is socially useful
- Interaction with other people
- Good wages

What do *you* want from *your* job?

What an Employer Wants

What an employer wants includes the training, skills, and work habits of workers. Employers want workers who will get to work on time and do their work well. Most employers also want workers who can get along well with other people.

There are a few employers around who don't want much from their employees. They'll take high school dropouts who have few skills. These employers don't pay much, either.

Most employers want employees with an education. Staying in school not only improves your chances of getting a job. It means you are likely to get a better job with better pay than if you drop out.

What an employer wants may also be determined by the employer's attitude about certain of a worker's personal characteristics. Such things as your age, your sex, or your race may help you get a certain job. Or they may make it very hard for you to get a certain job. There are laws that are supposed to limit an employer's discriminating against a worker on the basis of age, sex, or race—but they don't always work.

The Condition of the Labor Market

The condition of the labor market includes:

- How many jobs of a certain type are available?
- How many people with the proper skills are looking for jobs?
- What is the cost of labor?

If there are more jobs open than there are workers who have the skills to fill those jobs—that is, if there is a **shortage of workers**—your chances for getting a job are good.

If there are very few jobs and many workers looking for those jobs—that is, if there is a **surplus of workers**—you may not find any job.

The **cost of labor**—that is, what wages an employer must pay workers—influences the number of jobs available at any one time. If wages are high, employers will want to hire fewer workers. If wages are low, employers may be willing to hire more workers. Thus, the cost of labor influences who gets a job.

Answers to all of these three questions interact with each other. Let's look at three examples. Bob, Alice, and Larry, all high school graduates, applied for jobs at the Rollins Company.

Rollins' manager phoned the high school for references on the three applicants and found the following:

- Bob had a poor attendance record, was frequently late for school, and had poor to average grades.
- Carmen had a good attendance record, was never late, and had very good grades.
- Larry had a good attendance record and was seldom late. He had a C average.

Who do you think will get a job? It's hard to say until you have more information. What does the company want?

Suppose the Rollins Company needs 20 workers and has 50 applicants. They are likely to hire the 20 with the best records. This would include Carmen and probably Larry, but probably not Bob.

But suppose Rollins has only 20 applicants. If they want to fill all 20 positions, they might take a chance on Bob in spite of his poor school record.

As you see, finding an answer to "Who gets a job?" is not easy. Getting a job involves things which you can control—what you want from a job, your skills, and your work habits. Getting a job also involves things you cannot control—what the employer wants and the condition of the labor market.

2. A PICTURE OF THE U.S. WORK FORCE

Who Are U.S. Workers?

The following graphs will give you a picture of the U.S. work force. The work force includes all people 16 years old or over who—

- Have a job, or
- Are looking for a job.

Just over two-thirds of the U.S. population are in the work force—more than 127 million people.

Men and Women in the Work Force

Men are more likely to be in the work force than are women. Out of every 100 men who are 16 years old or older and not in school, 76 are in the work force. Out of every 100 women who are 16 years old or older and not in school, 58 are in the work force.

Figure 13–1 shows that men make up over half (55%) of the entire U.S. work force. Women make up 45% of the entire work force.

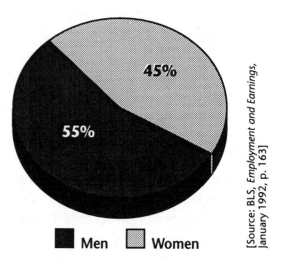

[Source: BLS, *Employment and Earnings*, January 1992, p. 163]

Figure 13–1 Percentage of Men and Women in the Work Force

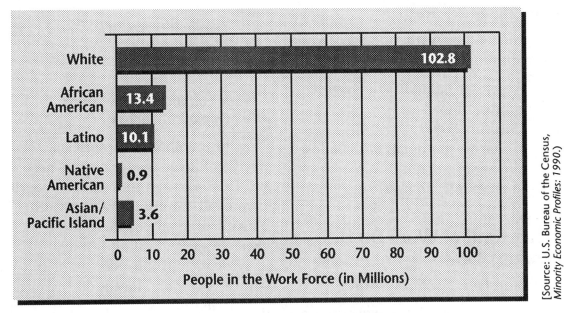

[Source: U.S. Bureau of the Census, *Minority Economic Profiles: 1990.*]

Figure 13–2 Number of People in the Work Force by Racial/Ethnic Group

Racial and Ethnic Groups in the U.S. Work Force

Figure 13–2 shows the number of whites, African Americans, Native Americans, Latinos, and Asian/Pacific Island Americans in the U.S. work force:

- 102.8 million whites
- 13.4 million African Americans
- 0.9 million Native Americans
- 10.1 million Latinos, and
- 3.6 million Asian/Pacific Islander Americans.

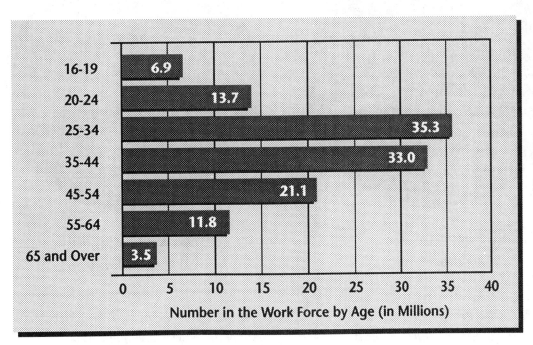

[Source: BLS, *Employment and Earnings,* January 1992, p. 164, 1991 Annual Data]

Figure 13–3 Number of People in the Work Force by Age

Age of the Work Force

Figure 13–3 shows the number of workers in different age groups.

- Which age group has the largest number of workers?
  (Answer: 25-34)
- Which age group has the smallest number of workers?
  (Answer: 65 and over)

What Kind of Work Do U.S. Workers Do?

Agricultural and Nonfarm Workers

Today few Americans work in agriculture. In the early days of our nation, more than 90 percent of the work force worked in agriculture.

Figure 13–4 shows the percent of U.S. workers today who work in agricultural jobs and those in nonfarm jobs.

> **Nonfarm jobs** = all jobs except those in farming and agriculture

Wage-Earning, Salaried, and Self-Employed Workers

The number of Americans who are self-employed today is very small.

In the mid-1800s most Americans were self-employed, many on farms. Less than half of all people in the work force were wage and salary workers.

Today only 10 percent of the work force is self-employed. Of these, 1% are in agriculture and 9% are in nonfarm businesses.

Figure 13–5 shows the percent of workers who are self-employed and the percent who receive wages or salaries from someone else.

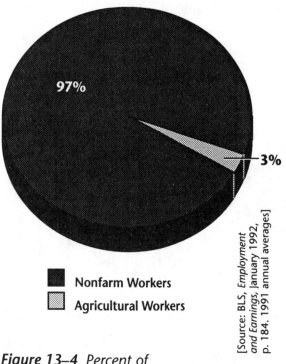

97%

3%

■ Nonfarm Workers

▨ Agricultural Workers

[Source: BLS, *Employment and Earnings*, January 1992, p. 184. 1991 annual averages]

Figure 13–4 *Percent of Agricultural and Nonfarm Workers in the United States*

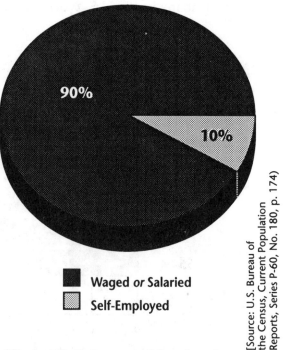

90%

10%

■ Waged *or* Salaried

▨ Self-Employed

[Source: U.S. Bureau of the Census, Current Population Reports, Series P-60, No. 180, p. 174)

Figure 13–5 *Percent of Employed Civilians who are Waged and Salaried and Those Who Are Self-Employed*

Workers in Service-Producing and Goods-Producing Industries

More than three and one-half times as many Americans work in service-producing industries as in goods-producing industries.

Jobs in goods-producing industries generally pay mid-level wages. A few pay rather high wages.

Service-producing industries have a small percentage of high-skill, high-wage jobs (such as computer programmers, technicians, and analysts) and a large percentage of low-skill, low-wage jobs (such as waiters, waitresses, retail clerks, and nurses' aides).

Goods-producing industries include:

- Mining
- Manufacturing
- Construction

Service-producing industries include:

- Transportation, communication, utilities
- Wholesale trade
- Retail trade
- Finance, insurance, and real estate
- Services—personal services, business and legal services, health services, education, religious organizations, child day care services, engineering and architectural services, repairs, recreation and amusements
- Government

Figure 13–6 shows the percentage of workers in goods-producing industries and in service-producing industries.

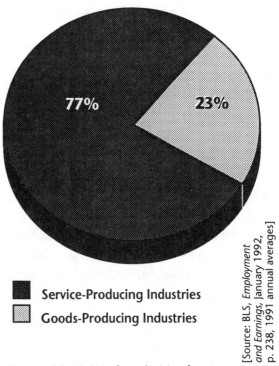

■ Service-Producing Industries
▨ Goods-Producing Industries

[Source: BLS, *Employment and Earnings,* January 1992, p. 238, 1991 annual averages]

Figure 13–6 *Workers in Nonfarm Industries by Type of Industry*

Jobs in the Future

During the last several years, a dramatic change has taken place in the kinds of jobs available to American workers. Many jobs in manufacturing were lost. Most of the new jobs that were created were in service-producing industries. Most of the new jobs paid less than the old jobs they replaced.

On the average, workers in the new jobs earned $7,039 less per year than workers in the old jobs. If you count fringe benefits such as health insurance and pension plans, the new jobs paid $10,404 less per year than the old jobs.

The U.S. Bureau of Labor Statistics expects that most of the new jobs added to the U.S. economy by the end of the century will be service-producing jobs. About half are expected to be in retail trade, private health services, and business services. Most will be low-skill, low-wage jobs with few fringe benefits.

By 2000, retail trade will employ more people than manufacturing and mining combined. One out of every 5 wage and salary jobs will be in retailing. In addition, there will be almost 2 million self-employed retailers.

Seven of the 10 fastest growing occupations between now and 2000 are in health services—medical assistants, home health aides, radiological technologists and technicians, medical records technicians, medical secretaries, physical therapists, and surgical technologists. One out of every 12 jobs in the year 2000 will be in health care.

Job Categories in the U.S. Work Force

The major job categories in the U.S. work force are:

- Executives and managers
- Professionals (such as doctors and lawyers)
- White-collar workers (technical, clerical and sales workers)
- Blue-collar workers (such as manufacturing and construction workers, truck drivers, and laborers)
- Agricultural workers (farming, fishing, and forestry workers)

Figure 13–7 shows the percent of workers in each type of work.

- Which job category has the greatest percentage of U.S. workers?
  (Answer: blue-collar workers)
- Which job category has the lowest percentage of U.S. workers?
  (Answer: farming, fishing, forestry)

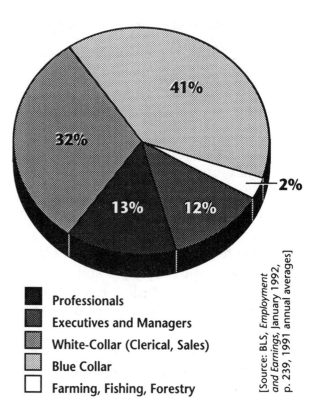

- ■ Professionals
- ▨ Executives and Managers
- ▥ White-Collar (Clerical, Sales)
- ▧ Blue Collar
- ☐ Farming, Fishing, Forestry

[Source: BLS, *Employment and Earnings*, January 1992, p. 239, 1991 annual averages]

Figure 13–7 *Percentage of Workers in Different Job Categories*

Think About It

1. Why do workers want to sell their labor?
2. Why do employers want to buy labor?
3. What effect does education have on getting a job?
4. In which category are most new jobs today, goods-producing industries or service-producing industries?

End of Chapter Quiz

Answer True (T) or False (F):

_____ 1. The *labor market* involves employers buying labor from workers.

_____ 2. Employers who hire high school dropouts usually don't pay very high wages.

_____ 3. It is easier to get a job when there is a surplus of workers than when there is a shortage of workers.

_____ 4. In general, employers will hire more workers when wages are high than when wages are low.

_____ 5. A higher percentage of men than of women are in the work force.

_____ 6. Today about half the people in the U.S. work force are self-employed.

_____ 7. Today the number of U.S. workers in goods-producing industries is about the same as the number in service-producing industries.

_____ 8. *Service-producing industries* include mining, manufacturing, and construction.

_____ 9. On the average, new jobs created over the last several years pay more than the jobs they replaced.

_____ 10. Most of the fastest growing occupations in the United States today are in health services.

CHAPTER 14

WHO DOESN'T HAVE A JOB?

1. UNEMPLOYMENT AND UNDEREMPLOYMENT

The Official Unemployment Rate

Not every worker who wants a job can find one. There are two kinds of people who are out of work:

- Officially unemployed workers, and
- Discouraged workers

Officially Unemployed Workers

The official number of unemployed includes people 16 years old and older who are not in school and who are looking for work. More than 9 million people are officially listed as unemployed.

The U.S. Department of Labor measures unemployment every month. The **official unemployment rate** is reported as a percentage of the work force. This rate changes from month to month. At the beginning of the 1990s this rate was 5.5% Since that time, the rate has often climbed much higher.

Discouraged Workers

In addition to the more than 9 million people on the official unemployment list in a recent month, almost 9 million other Americans wanted a job but had none. This group is sometimes called **discouraged workers**. Most of the people in this group have given up looking for work because of a lack of jobs in the job market or because of their own lack of skills.

Because these discouraged workers are not presently looking for work, they are not included in the official list. If they were added to the official list, the unemployment rate would be much higher.

Who Are the Unemployed?

Not all groups of Americans have the same chance of being unemployed. Some groups are much more likely to be unemployed than are other groups. In particular, members of the following groups are more likely to be unemployed:

- Minorities
- Young People

Minorities

Figure 14–1, at the top of the next page, is a recent graph of the unemployment rate by race.

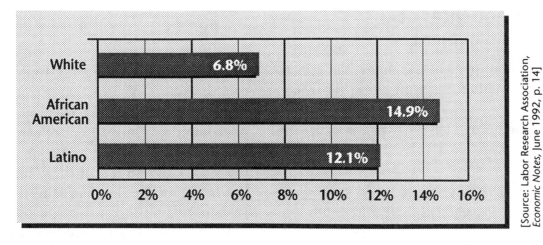

Figure 14–1 *Unemployment by Race*

Notice that African Americans are more than two times as likely to be unemployed as whites. Latinos are almost two times as likely to be unemployed as are whites.

Discrimination in hiring practices still plays a part in the high unemployment rates of minorities, even though such discrimination is now illegal. However, the present effects of past discrimination are also important. People who were denied jobs in the past because of discrimination lived in poverty. Children of poor families frequently receive poor educations, and thus have fewer skills. They also have less knowledge of job opportunities and of ways to prepare themselves for work.

Young People

Young workers are much more likely to be unemployed than are older workers. Minority youth are the most likely to be unemployed.

Figure 14–2 is a picture of unemployment of 16-19 year-olds. (Unemployment figures for Latino teenagers are not available.)

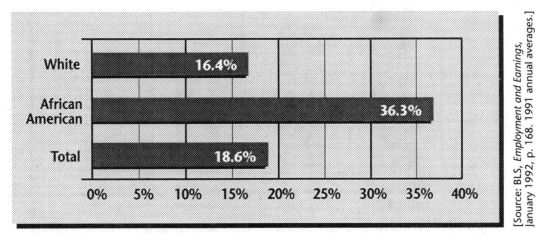

Figure 14–2 *Unemployment of 16-19 Year-Olds by Race*

Consequences of Unemployment

Unemployment has many bad effects on individuals as well as on the economy.

Unemployment is a major cause of poverty.

> **Poverty** = not enough money for the basic needs of life

We also use the word *poor* to refer to people in poverty.

Figure 14–3 is a picture of employment and unemployment for the heads of poverty and nonpoverty families.

The first two bars represent nonpoverty families. The heads of 81 out of every 100 nonpoverty families had a job at some time during the year; 61 out of every hundred worked full-time, year-round.

The second set of two bars represents poor families. Only 50 out of every 100 heads of poor families had a job during the year. Only 16 out of every hundred heads of poor families had a full-time job year-round.

With no jobs, unemployed people have trouble providing for their own needs. Many must rely on relatives, charity, or the government for support.

Today, large numbers of unemployed people are homeless, living on the streets of cities across the United States.

Unemployed people cannot contribute to the economy. They are not producing goods or services, and they have little money to buy goods or services.

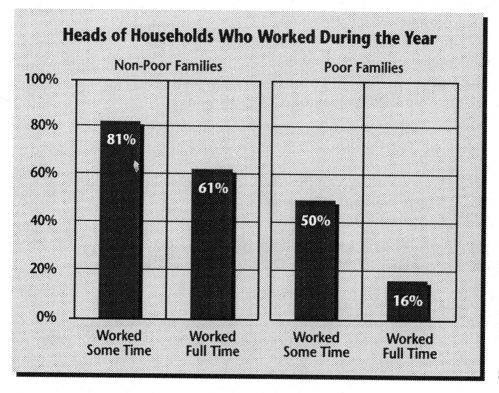

[Source: U.S. Bureau of the Census, Current Population Reports, Series P-60, No. 180, p. xv]

Figure 14–3 Percentage of Heads of Households Working During the Year

Being unemployed also affects people's physical and mental health. In fact, joblessness has been described as a demoralizing, wasting disease. Many jobless people suffer from malnutrition, lose their self-confidence, and become suicidal.

Underemployment: The Working Poor

Not all poor people are unemployed. Some have part-time jobs, and some have full-time jobs that pay very low wages. These people are called **underemployed.**

The **underemployed** include:

- Part-time workers who want full-time work but cannot find it
- Workers making very low wages
- Workers who can only find jobs below their skill and ability level

Underemployed workers are not included in official unemployment figures. However, they are a major part of the work force. For example, more than 5 million part-time workers want full-time jobs but cannot find them.

The wages of most underemployed workers are not high enough to keep them above the poverty level. This is true even when they work full time at minimum wages. For example, a full-time worker earning the minimum wage earns $170 per week. Working all 52 weeks during the year, this worker would earn less than $9,000. This income is too small to provide for all of his or her needs.

In a recent survey, half of the homeless people in New York City were working full time at minimum-wage jobs. They were homeless because their income was too low to pay for housing plus food.

2. CAUSES OF UNEMPLOYMENT AND UNDEREMPLOYMENT

What Causes Unemployment and Underemployment?

Some of the reasons why people have no jobs or inadequate jobs are:

- Lack of education
- No skills
- No knowledge of job opportunities
- No knowledge of ways to prepare oneself for work

Lack of Education and Unemployment

In general, the more education a person has, the higher that person's chance is of having a job. A good education does not guarantee a job, but if you have a good education, you will have more flexibility in the labor market. You will qualify for more different kinds of jobs and have more to offer an employer.

In a recent month the unemployment rate for all high school dropouts was 40 percent. This was *five times* the unemployment rate for the entire population at that time.

In a recent year, 40 percent of high school dropouts between the ages of 16 and 24 were not even in the labor force. Remember: the labor force includes only those who have a job or are actively looking for work. People who have given up looking for a job are not counted in either the labor force or the unemployment rate.

Figure 14–4 shows the unemployment rates for males and females 16 to 24 years old with different levels of education.

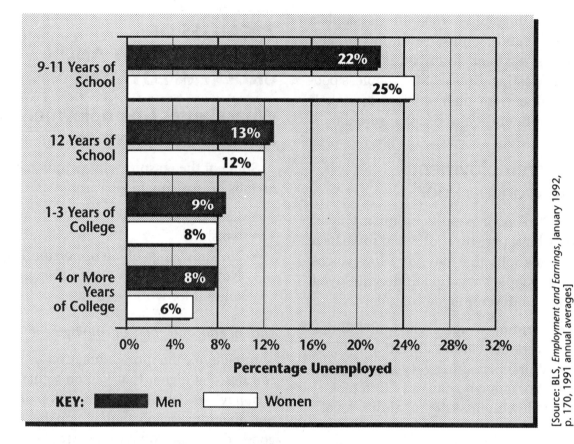

[Source: BLS, *Employment and Earnings*, January 1992, p. 170, 1991 annual averages]

Figure 14–4 *Unemployment Rates by Education Levels*

Remember that these unemployment rates are for people between the ages of 16 and 24 years old.

Notice that the unemployment rate is nearly two times higher for males who are not high school graduates (22%) than it is for males who have a high school diploma (13%). The unemployment rate for females who are not high school graduates (25%) is more than two times higher than it is for females who have a high school diploma (12%).

One to three years of education beyond high school lowers the unemployment rate even further, to 9% for males and to 8% for females. A college degree brings the rate down to 8% for males and to 6% for females.

Unemployment Among Qualified Workers

Many workers who have an education and good job skills are unemployed or underemployed. We have already noted that some people are unemployed because of discrimination.

Other reasons for unemployment have to do with—

- Workers entering or re-entering the labor market
- Changes in workers' job preferences
- Changes in the seasons or the weather
- Changes in industry and technology
- A decline in the growth of the nation's economy

Worker-Related Causes: Frictional Unemployment

Workers entering or re-entering the work force are counted as unemployed until they find a job. Examples are recent high school or college graduates and women who decide to get a job after raising their children. This kind of unemployment is usually temporary and is called **frictional unemployment.**

Changes in workers' job preferences can also cause temporary (frictional) unemployment between the time workers leave one job and find a new job.

Seasonal and Weather Causes: Seasonal Unemployment

Changes in the seasons and the weather create **seasonal unemployment.**

Farm workers, outdoor construction workers, and workers in the tourist industry are some of the groups affected by seasonal unemployment.

Seasonal unemployment is predictable. It occurs every year, regardless of changes in workers' job preferences, technology, the structure of industry, or how slowly the economy is growing.

Changes in Industry and Technology: Structural Unemployment

The development of new technologies changes the types of jobs that are available. Some industries disappear. New industries develop.

New industries and new technologies permanently change the types of jobs that are available. Unemployment caused by these permanent changes is called **structural unemployment.** Structural unemployment tends to affect large groups of

workers. It is much more serious than frictional or seasonal unemployment.

The candle-making industry declined when gas lights were developed. Later, the gas-light industry was replaced when electric lights were developed.

The development of farm machinery left many farm laborers unemployed but created manufacturing jobs. Jobs for carriage makers and blacksmiths disappeared when automobiles were developed. More recently, thousands of auto workers have lost jobs as the U.S. auto industry has declined.

When an entire industry dies or declines, there is no market for the skills of large numbers of workers. In such cases, workers must learn new skills or face long-term unemployment.

Slow Economic Growth: Cyclical Unemployment

Unemployment increases when the growth rate of the nation's economy slows down. As sales begin to drop, production slows down and workers are laid off.

At some times, the U.S. economy grows at a rapid rate. At other times, economic growth slows down. These periods make up the **business cycle** (the ups and downs of the economy).

Business cycles of slower and more rapid growth occur rather regularly in our economy. Unemployment that follows business cycles is called **cyclical unemployment.**

You read about business cycles in Chapter 3. Figure 14–5, on the next page, illustrates some of the up-and-down phases of the business cycle.

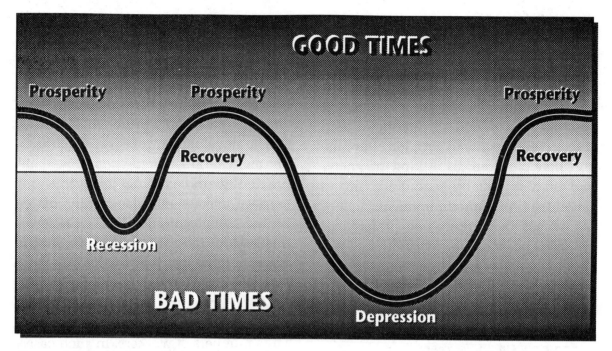

Figure 14–5 *Business Cycles*

The four basic phases of the business cycle are **Prosperity, Recession, Depression,** and **Recovery.**

- During times of **prosperity**, both sales and employment are high.
- During **recessions**, sales drop, production slows down, and workers are laid off.
- A return to prosperity is called a **recovery**.
- A recession that lasts very long or is very bad is called a **depression.**

Think About It

1. What groups are included in the *official unemployment rate?*
2. Name two groups that are especially likely to be unemployed.
3. Listen to news reports and read the newspaper to find out what the current unemployment rate is.
4. What are *discouraged workers?*
5. What is meant by *underemployment?*
6. What is the relationship between education and unemployment?
7. Give two reasons for unemployment among workers who have good job skills.

End of Chapter Quiz

Answer True (T) or False (F):

_____ 1. The *official unemployment rate* includes all people who want a job and don't have a job.

_____ 2. The term *discouraged workers* refers to those who have given up looking for a job.

_____ 3. The unemployment rate among African and Latino Americans is higher than among whites.

_____ 4. The unemployment rate is about the same for young workers as for older workers.

_____ 5. Unemployment is a major cause of poverty.

_____ 6. A person working full-time at minimum wage will earn enough to support a family of four above the poverty level.

_____ 7. Almost no homeless people have jobs.

_____ 8. Unemployment rates for high school dropouts are greater than for high school graduates.

_____ 9. Unemployment that is caused by changes in technology is called *cyclical unemployment.*

_____ 10. Unemployment for qualified workers increases during times of slow economic growth.

CHAPTER 15 WORKER ORGANIZATIONS

Adam Smith, the Scottish economist who supported economic freedom in the marketplace, wrote that a nation's wealth lies in its people and their labor.

Nearly all the labor that built the United States economy came from outside U.S. boundaries. Some workers came by choice; others were brought by force.

The history of American workers is a history of many groups of people including—

- *European immigrants*—Including self-employed farmers and workers, wage workers, and indentured servants who were bound by contract to work for an employer for a certain number of years.
- *Latin Americans*—Both natives of the Southwest at the time this area was annexed, and later immigrants.
- *Asians*—Brought over by labor contracts.
- *African Americans*—Originally captured in Africa, enslaved, and brought to this country, but a free people for more than 125 years.
- *Native Americans*—the one group of workers that did not originate outside the United States.

Workers and Employers

Most workers in the United States work for someone else. Only a very small percent are self-employed.

In the American business system, individuals are generally free to decide for whom they will work. You are limited, of course, by the number of companies that are hiring in your area. If you live in a small town that is dominated by a single company, finding another employer may take a long time and be quite costly. Workers may have to move to another town or city to find a job.

Employers are generally free to hire whomever they want—with a few exceptions. Child labor laws prevent employers from hiring children. Anti-discrimination laws make it illegal for employers to refuse to hire people on the basis of their race or sex.

As individuals, workers do not have much power when dealing with employers. In most cases, employers, not workers, decide on wages, work hours, and working conditions. The only way for most workers to have any power when dealing with employers is to organize into groups. Acting together as a group increases workers' ability to improve their wages and working conditions.

At first there were no formal organizations of workers. Later, in response to harsh working conditions, workers began joining together in unions to fight for their rights.

1. THE HISTORY OF THE UNION MOVEMENT

Early Unions

Very few unions existed before the Civil War. One reason was that only a small part of the population worked in factories. Most people were farmers working on small farms or owners of small businesses. For the most part, the U.S. legal system did not support unions before the Civil War.

The first unions that were formed before the Civil War did not have much success in improving the lives of workers. Certain conditions of the times worked together to keep these early unions weak and ineffective:

- Many workers in that period were indentured servants who were forbidden to form or join unions.
- Many new immigrants were coming to the United States. When unionized workers demanded better wages and working conditions, employers could replace them with these new immigrants.
- When unionized workers demanded better wages or shorter hours, employers could replace them with children or women. Children had no unions, and women were not allowed to join most unions.

- Many workers were slaves. There were no unions on the cotton plantations in the South. The existence of cheap slave labor also helped keep wages low for workers elsewhere. Even when they bargained as a group, free workers had little power with their employer if the employer's competitor could produce the same goods cheaper with slave labor.

For all of these reasons, early unions were weak, and most lasted only a short time. Wages and working conditions for most workers did not improve.

Industrial Growth after the Civil War

After the Civil War, industry grew rapidly. Competition was intense. In order to keep profits high, industrialists and factory owners kept production costs, including labor costs, as low as possible. This meant low wages, long hours, and poor working conditions. Factories were dangerous, unsanitary, and noisy. Working days were long; 12- to 14-hour work days were common. In some factories, children worked from 6 a.m. until midnight for three dollars a week. Most workers lived in extreme poverty. During this period, employers actively recruited southern and eastern European and Mexican immigrants so that they would have plenty of cheap labor.

Rapid industrial growth did not create a stable economy. Periodic overproduction meant more goods were produced than could be sold (surpluses). Prices fell, and huge numbers of workers lost their jobs as factories shut down.

Given these conditions of poverty and unemployment, workers sought to improve their conditions by organizing themselves. In the years following the Civil War, many new unions were formed and their membership grew rapidly.

Goals of the Labor Movement

During this period, the labor movement was divided by a major conflict over its goals.

- Some believed that unions should focus on improving the day-to-day lives of workers—higher wages, shorter hours, better working conditions, and job security.
- Others felt that this was not enough. They believed that the economic system itself needed to be changed.

Those who wanted changes in the basic economic system believed it was wrong for a few very powerful people (industrialists or the owners of factories and businesses who are called **capitalists**) to tell workers what to do and get rich from the labor of workers. They believed that each industry should be owned by the workers who built it or by the public, not by a few individuals.

Most employers disagreed with both kinds of labor organizers. They were extremely hostile to the unions and refused to bargain with workers.

A major strategy of unions during this period was the **strike**, which aimed at gaining employer concessions.

❖ **Strike** = an organized work stoppage. Unions use strikes as a way to pressure an employer to meet the demands of the union

In response to union strikes, big business hired private police forces or mobilized **vigilantes** to attack striking union workers.

❖ **Vigilantes** = an unofficial group that punishes people without the authority of law or the courts

Workers and sometimes their wives and children were killed in bloody attacks. Between the 1870s and the 1930s, more than 700 workers were killed in labor struggles.

Rather than give in to union demands, employers often hired other workers, called **strikebreakers**, to take the jobs of striking union members.

Faced with employer violence, labor could rarely turn to government for protection. In general, government protected neither the workers' rights to unionize nor their physical safety. Often the National Guard or federal troops were called out against striking workers. Court decisions also favored business over unions.

Although there was less violence on the part of workers than on the part of business, workers sometimes engaged in sabotage directed at company property. Workers also attacked strikebreakers, whom they called **scabs.**

Unions of Skilled Workers

Skilled craftsmen formed the first labor unions in the United States. These unions followed the goal of changing working conditions rather than changing the economic system. They sought shorter work hours and higher wages. It was their policy not to get involved in politics.

The AFL

In 1886 the **American Federation of Labor (AFL)** was founded, bringing together local unions of skilled workers, called **craft unions.** For the most part, the AFL excluded women, African Americans, and unskilled workers.

Workers in Mass Production

The Industrial Revolution had changed the way in which most goods were produced. Manufacturing was broken down into small tasks. Each worker was responsible for only one small part of the manufacturing process. Highly skilled workers were no longer needed in most industries. Unskilled workers made up a growing proportion of the labor force.

These unskilled workers were poorly paid. Working conditions in large manufacturing plants were dangerous and often inhumane. Eventually, the millions of unskilled workers who were left out of the AFL formed unions of their own.

The IWW

The **Industrial Workers of the World (IWW)** was formed in 1905. Its members, nicknamed **Wobblies**, were mostly unskilled workers.

The goal of the IWW was to create a new society based on worker control of industry. It took a militant stand in favor of workers' rights. Mass strikes were organized in textile mills, iron and copper mines, lumber towns, and harvest fields. Other strategies of the IWW included **wildcat strikes**, work slowdowns, and some **sabotage.**

❖ *Wildcat strike = a spontaneous strike not authorized by union leaders*

❖ *Sabotage = damage done by workers to machines or to products*

IWW strikes were violently opposed by company vigilantes, local police forces, and the National Guard.

It was the policy of the IWW to stay independent of political parties. Although they were sympathetic to the Communist revolution in Russia (1917), the Wobblies opposed the centralized, totalitarian government which developed there. Nevertheless, IWW members were accused of being spies of the Soviet Union. Government as well as business opposition to the IWW was intense. Some IWW leaders were lynched, and thousands of members were jailed. Hundreds of immigrant workers were deported without due process of law. By the mid-1920s, the IWW was destroyed.

Union Growth during the Great Depression

The worst depression in the history of the United States began in 1929. By 1933, production was less than one-third of what it had been before the Depression. Wages were extremely low, and millions of workers were unemployed.

During this period, labor organizing increased in mass-production industries, which employed mostly unskilled and semi-skilled workers. Many workers went on strike for better conditions and to force employers to recognize the unions. Militant union members included both political radicals (like most former IWW members) and those who were only interested in better pay and working conditions.

As in earlier years, business resisted unionization, and again many violent clashes took place between strikers and the police.

The CIO

In 1935, union militants formed the Committee of Industrial Organizations to unite the unskilled and semiskilled workers who had been ignored by the AFL. Three years later this Committee became the **Congress of Industrial Organizations (CIO).**

Unlike AFL unions, which were typically small craft unions of white male workers, CIO unions were typically large. They represented such industries as steel, automobiles, rubber, and chemicals. They also included women, African-Americans, and other minorities. These unions included workers who did all the various jobs within a particular industry.

The CIO also was more politically involved than the AFL. CIO unions supported the Democratic party and were interested in more issues than just the day-to-day welfare of workers.

In 1930, only about 11% of the nation's non-farm workers were union members. By 1945, this proportion had grown to more than 35%.

Sit-Down Strikes

In the union struggles of the 1930s, sit-down strikes were a major tactic for gaining employer recognition of industrial unions. Workers stopped work, sat down in the plant, and refused to leave until employers agreed to grant the rights they sought.

Sit-down strikes were effective because employers could not bring in strikebreakers without removing the workers by force.

And using force inside the plant would damage the company's equipment.

In the summer of 1936, hundreds of Michigan auto workers died in a period of four days while forced to work in unventilated plants in over 100 degrees heat. The rest of the auto workers staged a sit-down strike. Workers' wives brought food to the windows of the plant even though police used tear gas against them. On one day, the police shot 14 women.

After 44 days, the employer, General Motors, recognized the union and began meeting some of the workers' demands.

New Kinds of Unions

Since the 1960s there has been a significant increase in the numbers and strength of two kinds of unions. These are

- White collar unions, and
- Farm workers' unions

White-Collar Unions

In the last thirty years or so, white collar unions—especially those representing teachers, government workers, and clerical workers—have grown in power. The growth of these unions indicates the increasing importance of service jobs compared with manufacturing jobs in the U.S. economy.

The Farm Workers' Union

The **United Farm Workers of America (UFW)** is one of the most successful farm workers' unions in U.S. history. It was organized in the 1960s to help migrant farm workers. Migrant workers are workers, mostly Hispanic people in California, who move from farm to farm picking crops as they become ready for harvest. In the late 1960s, migrant farm workers' wages ranged between $1.07 and $1.70 per hour. Most lived in seriously inadequate housing with little or no sanitation facilities. The UFW has worked to improve conditions for farm workers. When growers refused to talk with the union, farm workers picketed and were fired upon.

Farm workers have a high rate of disabling injuries, especially from pesticide poisoning. The UFW is now campaigning to stop the use of pesticides that poison consumers as well as farm workers.

---

2. LABOR CONTRACTS

When you take a job, you enter into a **contract** with your employer. You agree to do certain work under certain conditions in exchange for a certain amount of pay and perhaps certain other benefits such as health insurance or a pension plan.

❖ *Contract = A legal agreement. Contracts are enforceable by law*

Collective Bargaining

Collective bargaining is a process in which union officials meet with company officials to work out an agreement on wages and working conditions. When all union members bargain together through their representatives, workers have a stronger voice than each worker would have bargaining as an individual with the company.

The object of collective bargaining is to work out a contract. Although business violently opposed unions from the start, contracts with labor unions have a major advantage for business. By agreeing to a contract, employers gain labor peace for the period covered by the contract.

By signing a contract, workers may gain wage or other benefits but they generally agree not to protest during the life of the contract. One reason why businesses hated the IWW so much was that the IWW refused to sign contracts. "We renegotiate every day" was the policy of IWW unions.

In reality, both employers and workers often violate the terms of contracts, leading to renewed conflict. Wildcat strikes occur when workers take action against their employers over contract violations.

What happens if business and labor cannot agree on a contract? Several things are possible:

- The union may **strike** (refuse to work) until a settlement is reached.
- The company may try a **lockout**. It locks the workers out until a settlement is reached.
- The two sides may ask a third party to help them find a solution. Sometimes the third party is a **mediator** who gives both sides advice. Neither side is bound to follow a mediator's advice.

  Other times the third party is an **arbitrator**. Both sides must agree in advance to accept the decision of an arbitrator.
- The government may take steps to keep the plant open if it believes a work stoppage would create a national emergency.

Three such government actions are:

- The government may order the two sides to submit to arbitration.
- The courts may issue an injunction—a legal command ordering the union not to strike or ordering the employer not to lock employees out.
- The government may take over a plant and run it temporarily until an agreement is worked out.

3. LABOR LEGISLATION

Since 1933, several federal laws have been passed relating to unions.

The National Industrial Recovery Act

In order to help stabilize the economy, and because of pressure from unions, Congress passed the **National Industrial Recovery Act (NIRA)** in 1933. This act legally protected the right of industrial workers to organize unions.

The Wagner Act

Because violence by employers against unions continued, unions pressured Congress to pass a stronger law. In 1935, Congress passed the **National Labor Relations Act,** known as the **Wagner Act** from the name of the Senator who sponsored it. The Wagner Act required employers to recognize and bargain with unions. The Act set up a National Labor Relations Board to handle complaints about unfair labor practices.

Fair Labor Standards Act

In 1938, Congress passed the **Fair Labor Standards Act,** sometimes called the **Wages and Hours Law.** This act—

- Restricted child labor
- Set a minimum wage
- Set a maximum work week
- Guaranteed that workers would be paid time-and-a-half pay for overtime hours

The work week was set at 44 hours, but this was later lowered to 40 hours.

The Taft-Hartley Act

The Wagner Act was passed because of pressure from ordinary American workers during the Great Depression. During World War II, business leaders agreed to honor workers' rights in exchange for labor peace. Following the war, however, many business leaders backed off from their cooperation with labor and supported anti-labor policies.

Anti-labor policies became law in the Taft-Hartley Act, passed in 1947. The act severely weakened unions by—

- Outlawing the "closed shop," which prevented a business from hiring non-union members
- Giving states the right to pass "right-to-work" laws outlawing the "union shop," which required new workers to join the union
- Restricting union bargaining strategies
- Requiring unions to give 60-days notice before striking
- Outlawing union contributions to political candidates
- Increasing government control over unions

Weakening Union Power over Hiring

The Taft-Hartley Act attacked the security of unions by outlawing the closed shop and by giving states the right to pass right-to-work laws.

In a **closed shop**, a business can hire only union members. This type of contract gives the union the greatest protection from destruction by employees. Because unions can control who becomes a union member, they also control who is hired in a closed shop.

Unions in some states can still make **union shop** contracts. A union shop is a business in which all new employees must join the union, although new employees don't have to be union members before they are hired. However, the Taft-Hartley Act gave states the right to outlaw union shops by passing right-to-work laws. In states that have passed **right-to-work laws,** employers have the right to hire either union or nonunion workers. New employees are not required to join the union. Such businesses are called **open shops.**

Prohibiting Secondary Boycotts

The Taft-Hartley Act restricted unions' bargaining tactics in other ways. For example, it prohibited mass picketing. It also prohibited unions from organizing secondary boycotts.

❖ **Boycott = a refusal to deal with some group**

Union action directed at an employer—striking, picketing, refusing to buy the company's products—is a **primary boycott.** Similar actions against companies that do business with the employer is a **secondary boycott.** Unions had used secondary boycotts to force other companies to put pressure for a settlement on a stubborn employer. These secondary boycotts were forbidden by the Taft-Hartley act.

Increasing Government Control of Unions

The Taft-Hartley Act increased government's control over unions by giving the President of the United States power to ask the courts to delay a strike for 80 days if the strike would create a national emergency.

Effects of the Taft-Hartley Act

Since the passage of the Taft-Hartley Act, unions have lost both strength and members. Some of this is caused by the weakening of union power by the act. Some is due to the decline in importance of manufacturing in the United States, since many manufacturing jobs have moved overseas.

Today, less than 20 percent of the nonfarm labor force are union members. Many of these belong to unions of government workers. In private industry, only about 12% of the workers belong to unions. This is the lowest rate among major industrialized countries.

Benefits of Labor Unions

The labor movement has brought significant benefits to both union and nonunion workers in the United States. Improvements have been made in work place safety. The 40-hour week is now standard. Workers have more job security because of **seniority** practices. This means that workers who have been with a company the longest, that is, have the greatest seniority, will be the last to be fired during layoffs.

Most workers are covered by the minimum wage law. Wages for nonunion workers in many companies are higher now because of the influence of union negotiations with other companies.

4. LABOR PROBLEMS TODAY

Declining Power of Unions

The power of workers compared with employers is declining today.

Some employers hire union-busting firms to keep unions out of their plants. There are about 1500 such union-busting firms in the United States. Employers have paid as much as $300,000 to such a firm to keep from raising workers' wages from $4.00 to $4.24 per hour.

Some employers fight striking workers by replacing them permanently with nonunion workers. This tactic became especially important in the 1980s and 1990s. Unions are working for laws that would forbid this practice.

In the early 1980s and again in the 1990s, unemployment rates rose. Many union workers were forced to accept wage and benefit cuts because of nationwide recessions.

Union Corruption

Corruption and authoritarian practices by some union leaders have caused many members to lose faith in their unions. In the 1970s and 1980s a number of reform organizations, such as Steelworkers Fight Back and Teamsters for a Democratic Union, have fought for more democratic unions. (Teamsters are truck drivers.)

Plant Closings

Plant closings are another major problem facing U.S. workers today. Between 1981 and 1986, nearly 11 million workers lost jobs because of plant closings or employment cutbacks. Many of these workers were given no notice. When a large employer leaves an area, there are seldom enough other jobs for the unemployed workers.

A variety of industries, including computers, electronics, data processing, clothing and shoe manufacturing, have relocated to less developed places and countries such as Puerto Rico, Thailand, Taiwan, and Hong Kong. Most workers there are not organized, and wages are as low as $.50 to $1.50 an hour. Many of these areas have laws restricting unions.

Plant closings affect the economy of the whole community. When large numbers of jobs disappear, unemployed workers have little money to pay for housing, food, clothing, or other goods. Local businesses suffer. Even community services such as schools face budget problems because of loss of taxes.

In recent years workers have tried to get laws passed that would require employers to give advance warning when plants are to be closed so that they can find other jobs. So far they have not succeeded. In 1988 Congress passed a bill requiring stable companies that know in advance of plans for closing plants or laying off workers to share this information with workers and local governments 60 days in advance. However, the bill was vetoed by President Reagan.

Fair Pay

The average working woman's pay today is about two-thirds that of a man's. Some reasons for this are:

- Women have been excluded from most unions.
- Women have been excluded from many higher paying jobs.
- Women are concentrated in certain "female" jobs that pay less than traditionally "male" jobs.

The **Equal Pay Act** (1963) requires that men and women who do the same job must be paid the same. But this law says nothing about equal rates of pay for different jobs that require similar skill and responsibility levels.

Figure 15–1 below gives an example of this difference. The information is from a recent Boston, Massachusetts, wage survey. The chart shows average hourly wages for four occupations: registered nurse, auto mechanic, truck driver, and electrical maintenance worker. Most registered nurses are women. Most workers in the other three jobs are men.

Wages for the three mostly-male occupations are significantly higher than for the mostly-female occupation.

Job Title	Average Hourly Wage
Registered Nurse	$ 12.42
Auto Mechanic	13.34
Truck Driver	13.65
Electrical Maintenance Worker	13.78

Figure 15–1 Average Hourly Wage of Four Jobs

Today many workers support a policy of **comparable worth.** "Comparable worth" means paying the same wages for jobs that require similar levels of skill and responsibility, no matter if workers are mostly men or mostly women.

Health and Safety Problems

Working conditions in many industries, such as mining, construction, transportation, manufacturing, textiles, and meat packing, are still dangerous. Pressure in many industries to work faster contributes to death and accident rates. In one recent year, a total of almost 6.6 million work-related illnesses and injuries were reported. Eighty-six on-the-job injuries or deaths were reported for every 1000 full-time workers.

Think About It

1. During what period of American history did unions first begin to grow rapidly?
2. What two major labor movement goals caused conflict among unions in the early period of union growth?
3. What is the purpose of *strikes?*
4. What is a *contract?*
5. Give three of the provisions of the Fair Labor Standards Act of 1938.
6. Why are plant closings a problem for workers in the United States today?
7. What is meant by a policy of *comparable worth?*

End of Chapter Quiz

Answer True (T) or False (F):

_____ 1. In most workplaces in the United States today, workers and employers have equal say in deciding on wages, work hours, and working conditions.

_____ 2. The only way for most workers to have any power when dealing with employers is to organize into groups.

_____ 3. Several strong labor unions were formed in the United States before the Civil War.

_____ 4. During the industrial boom that followed the Civil War, many children worked in dangerous factories from 6 a.m. until midnight for very low wages.

_____ 5. The rapid industrialization following the Civil War created a stable economy.

_____ 6. Following the Civil War, the labor movement was united in its goals to change the basic economic system in the United States.

_____ 7. A _strike_ is a work stoppage intended to force employers to meet workers' demands.

_____ 8. During the early days of the labor movement, big business often hired _vigilantes_ to attack striking union workers.

_____ 9. During the early days of the labor movement, government usually protected the workers' rights to form unions and their physical safety.

_____ 10. The first unions in the United States were formed by unskilled factory workers.

_____ 11. In general women were allowed to join the early labor unions, but African Americans were not.

_____ 12. The _IWW_ was originally a union of skilled crafts workers.

_____ 13. The _Great Depression_ of the 1930s was a time of union growth.

_____ 14. The _CIO_ was a group of large unions representing workers in major industries such as steel and automobiles.

(Continued on the next page)

End of Chapter Quiz (continued)

Answer True (T) or False (F):

____ 15. *Sit-down strikes* were effective because employers could not easily replace striking workers with strikebreakers.

____ 16. Since the 1960s, unions of clerical workers, teachers, and government workers have grown in numbers and in power.

____ 17. The major aim of the United Farm Workers of America has been to help migrant farm workers.

____ 18. A *contract* is a legal agreement that is enforceable by law.

____ 19. Labor unions use *collective bargaining* to work out a contract with employers.

____ 20. Contracts are almost never a benefit to employers.

____ 21. The *National Labor Relations Act*, passed in 1935, required employers to recognize and bargain with unions.

____ 22. Congress established the first *minimum wage* in 1910.

____ 23. The *Taft-Hartley Act* strengthened the power of unions.

____ 24. In the last several years, millions of U.S. workers have lost their jobs because employers have moved their plants to other countries where wages are lower than in the United States.

____ 25. The *Equal Pay Act* of 1963 requires employers to pay equal wages for different jobs that require a similar level of skill or responsibility.

CHAPTER 16

PAYING TAXES

Suppose you have a job. The first week at work you earn $150.00. When you get your first pay check, however, the amount you are paid is $133.73.

There must be some mistake with your pay check, you think. You were supposed to earn $150.00. What happened to the rest?

Let's look at the **pay stub**—a piece of paper attached to your check. It says:

GROSS PAY	FED TAX	FICA TAX	NET PAY
$150.00	5.00	11.27	$133.73

Your **gross pay** is the total amount you earned.

Your **net pay**, also called **take-home pay**, is the amount you actually receive.

Two Kinds Of Payroll Taxes

Your check is less than $150.00 because you paid two kinds of taxes:

- Income Tax and
- FICA (Social Security)

Income Tax

The first tax, called FED TAX on your pay stub, is **federal income tax.** This tax is withheld from workers' pay. You don't receive it. Your employer sends the tax to the Internal Revenue Service.

Almost half of the money used for federal government salaries and programs comes from personal income taxes. This is the largest single source of revenue for the federal government.

Income tax must be paid on wages. It also must be paid on interest and dividends earned from savings accounts and investments.

Many states have income taxes. If you live in a state like this, you will have the **state income tax** taken out of your pay, too.

Social Security Tax

The second tax, called FICA TAX on your pay stub, is usually called **Social Security tax.** (The initials **FICA** stand for **Federal Insurance Contributions Act**, the name of the law that set up this kind of tax.)

The Social Security tax pays for pensions and hospitalization insurance (Medicare) for retired workers and for workers who are permanently disabled.

Three Methods of Taxing

There are three basic methods of taxing:

- Progressive tax
- Regressive tax
- Proportional tax

Progressive Taxes

Progressive taxes use a lower rate for people with low incomes and a higher rate for people with high incomes. The federal income tax is a progressive tax. It increases in steps as income increases. For example:

- Family A had a taxable income of $10,000. They paid **15%** of that income in taxes ($1,500).
- Family B had a taxable income of $40,000. They paid **15%** tax on the first $30,950 and **28%** tax on the rest. They paid a total of $7,176 in taxes.
- Family C had a taxable income of $100,000. They paid **15%** tax on the first $30,905, **28%** tax on the next 43,900, and **33%** on the rest. Their total taxes were $25,234.

Regressive Taxes

Regressive taxes take a larger percent from low-income people and a smaller percent from high-income people. A sales tax is a regressive tax.

Suppose that a state has a 5% sales tax.

- A family with an income of $18,000 spends $9,000 on taxable goods. This means they pay $450 in sales tax. This is 2.5% of their total income.

- Another family with an income of $40,000 spends $15,000 on taxable items. They pay $750 in sales tax. This is 1.875% of this family's total income.

The lower-income family paid fewer dollars in sales tax, but it was a much higher percentage of their total income.

Proportional Taxes

Proportional taxes take the same percent from every taxpayer. Suppose the income tax rate was 22% for all taxpayers. Then—

- Family A earns $10,000 a year and pays $2,200 in taxes.
- Family B earns $40,000 a year and pays $8,800 in taxes.
- Family C earns $100,000 a year and pays $22,000 in taxes.

The three families pay different amounts, but the amount is **proportional** to the amount each family earns.

Which Type of Tax Is Most Fair?

From the viewpoint of ability to pay, which type of tax is the most fair?

It is easy to see that a regressive tax takes more from those who can least afford to pay. But what about the progressive and proportional taxes? Which of these is most fair?

Let's look at the three families in the above examples. Suppose the government needed to raise a total of $33,000 in taxes from Family A, Family B, and Family C.

How a Proportional Tax Affects the Three Families

First we will compare the amount of income tax each family would pay if we had a 22% *proportional* tax rate. That is, everyone, regardless of income, would pay 22% of their income in tax. In Figure 16–1, the last column on the right shows how much money each family would have left after paying the 22% tax.

Sure enough, at this tax rate, the government collects $33,000 in taxes.

How does this affect the three families?

- Family A pays far less in taxes than either Family B or Family C. However, since Family A had very little to start with, even this relatively small amount of tax is a significant portion of their income. They are left with only $7,700. This is not enough to meet their needs.
- Family B's taxes ($8,800) are also a substantial part of their income. But the $30,800 they have left is probably enough to meet most of their needs.
- Family C pays quite a lot in taxes. But they started with a very large income. Even after paying $22,000 in taxes they have $77,000 left. They can live quite well on this amount.

TAXPAYER	TAXABLE INCOME	AMOUNT OF TAX	AMOUNT LEFT
FAMILY A	$10,000	$2,200	$7,700
FAMILY B	$40,000	$8,800	$30,800
FAMILY C	$100,000	$22,000	$77,000
TOTAL TAXES COLLECTED:	**$33,000**		

Figure 16–1 *Proportional Tax of 22%*

How a Progressive Tax Affects the Three Families

Next, let's compare the amount of income tax each family would pay using a progressive tax. Remember, actual income tax rates are progressive. As income goes up, the tax rate also goes up. In Figure 16–2, the last column on the right shows how much money each family has left after taxes.

Under this progressive tax system, the government raises a bit more than under the proportional system.

- Family A's taxes are now only $1,500, although even this amount is a lot compared with their income. Still, they have more left than at the proportional tax rate of 22%.
- Family B pays $2,024 less in taxes under the progressive tax system. This extra money will make it easier for them to meet their needs.

TAXPAYER	TAXABLE INCOME	AMOUNT OF TAX	AMOUNT LEFT
FAMILY A	$10,000	$1,500	$8,500
FAMILY B	$40,000	$7,176	$32,824
FAMILY C	$100,000	$25,234	$74,766
TOTAL TAXES COLLECTED:		**$33,910**	

Figure 16–2 Progressive Tax

- Family C's taxes are $3,234 more than under the proportional system. Still, the $74,766 they have left will allow them to live very well.

Think About It

1. What is the difference between *gross* pay and *net* pay?
2. What is the more common name for FICA tax?
3. What is meant by a *progressive* tax?
4. What is meant by a *regressive* tax?
5. What is meant by a *proportional* tax?
6. Which type of tax do you think is the most fair, the *progressive* or the *proportional?* Explain your reasons.

End of Chapter Quiz

Answer True (T) or False (F):

_____ 1. For most workers, *net pay* is the same as *gross pay.*

_____ 2. Federal income tax and Social Security tax are both withheld from workers' paychecks.

_____ 3. Almost half the money used to run the federal government comes from personal income taxes.

_____ 4. *Social Security taxes* are used to pay for education programs.

_____ 5. *Take-home pay* is another term for *net pay.*

_____ 6. A *progressive tax* is figured at the same percentage for all taxpayers, no matter what their income is.

_____ 7. A *regressive tax* takes a lower percentage from people with low incomes and a higher percentage from people with high incomes.

_____ 8. A *proportional tax* takes more from low income people than from high income people.

_____ 9. In the United States today, the personal income tax is a *progressive tax.*

_____ 10. Since all states do not have a state income tax, this tax is never withheld from workers' paychecks.

CHAPTER 17 USING YOUR MONEY

1. ECONOMIC CHOICES

It's a great feeling to have your first pay check. But it won't take long to see that this wonderful check won't buy everything you want. You must make some decisions about how to spend your pay.

Alternative Costs

Deciding how to spend your money is an economic decision. No matter what you decide, you will be giving up something you want, at least for the present time. What you give up is called your **alternative cost** (also called **opportunity cost**).

- You want a new coat.
- You want a bike.
- You also want a ticket to a special concert.

You don't have enough money for all three. Your wants are greater than your resources. What will you do?

Here are some of your choices:

- Buy a bike.
- Buy a nice coat.
- Buy a cheaper coat and a concert ticket.

- See the concert and save buying the other things until your next pay check.

Here is what your decisions mean:

- If you buy a bike, you must keep your old coat and skip the concert.
- If you buy a good coat, you will have no bike. You will also have to skip the concert.
- If you go to the concert, you will not have money left over, but not enough money for a bike or a good coat. But you can buy a cheaper coat. Or, you can save your money until you have enough to buy both the bike and the coat you really want.

Which decision will give you the smallest alternative cost? It's a personal decision.

You must decide which item is most important to you—the bike, a nice coat, or the concert. Then you will know which things you would rather give up. You will know which choice will give you the smallest alternative cost.

2. SAVING MONEY

You've been working a year now. Every month you have put $50.00 into a savings account. In 12 months, you have saved $600.00.

But while you have been working, your savings have also been working—earning interest.

❖ **Interest** = *money earned by savings accounts*

The bank where you have your savings account pays 5.5% interest compounded monthly.

- An **interest rate of 5.5%** means that every dollar on deposit for a year earns 5.5 cents; $100 on deposit for one year earns $5.50. Interest paid this way is sometimes known as **simple interest.** If your account earned this kind of interest, you would end up with $616.50 at the end of the year. (Remember, you didn't have the whole $600 in the bank all year, so you don't get 5.5% on the whole $600.)

- **Interest compounded monthly—** the kind of interest your account is actually earning—means that one month's interest is paid to your account every month. This interest is added to your balance. The next month's interest is paid on your new balance (that is, your old balance *plus* the last month's interest). You end up with more interest at the end of the year because your balance grows every month.

This is what your savings account passbook looks like when interest is compounded monthly:

DATE	DEPOSIT	INTEREST	WITHDRAWAL	BALANCE
SEPT. 1	50.00	—	—	50.00
SEPT. 31	—	.23 INT	—	50.23
OCT. 1	50.00	—	—	100.23
OCT. 31	—	.47 INT	—	100.70
NOV. 1	50.00	—	—	150.70
NOV. 30	—	.68 INT	—	151.38
DEC. 1	50.00	—	—	201.38
DEC. 31	—	.91 INT	—	202.29
JAN. 1	50.00	—	—	252.29
JAN. 31	—	1.81 INT	—	253.47
FEB. 1	50.00	—	—	303.47
FEB. 28	—	1.28 INT	—	304.75
MAR. 1	50.00	—	—	354.75
MAR. 31	—	1.66 INT	—	356.41

(Continued on the next page)

DATE	DEPOSIT	INTEREST	WITHDRAWAL	BALANCE
APR. 1	50.00	—	—	406.41
APR. 30	—	1.84 INT	—	408.25
MAY 1	50.00	—	—	458.25
MAY 31	—	2.14 INT	—	460.39
JUNE 1	50.00	—	—	510.39
JUNE 30	—	2.31 INT	—	512.70
JULY 1	50.00	—	—	562.70
JULY 31	—	2.63 INT	—	565.33
AUG. 1	50.00	—	—	615.33
AUG. 31	—	2.87 INT	—	618.20

Figure 17–1 Sample ledger from a savings account

3. CREDIT: GETTING A BANK LOAN

You now have $618.20 in your savings account. You want to buy a used car. But $618.20 isn't enough. You could wait a year or two until you've saved some more, but you need the car now.

One answer might be to buy the car on **credit**.

❖ **Credit** = buying a product now and paying for it later

Why not get a loan? You've never had a loan before. Will the bank give you a loan?

- Getting a loan is one way of **buying on credit**.

You decide to talk to the loan officer at your bank. You explain that the car you want costs $1500. You ask if you can get a loan for $1000.

The loan officer asks you to fill out an application. She checks with your employer to be sure you have the job you list on the application. She asks your employer how much you earn and if he plans to keep you as an employee.

The bank's interest rate for car loans is 8%.

❖ **Interest** = The amount borrowers have to pay for the use of borrowed funds

The interest rate on a car loan is 2.5% more than the interest your savings earn. The bank charges more interest than it pays in order to pay its expenses and also make a profit.

The loan officer explains that if you take the loan you will have to repay it at the rate of $55 every month plus $7.22 a month interest. Your loan will be for 18 months. You will have 17 monthly payments of $62.22 and one final payment of $62.26. At the end of the 18 months, the car will belong to you.

The loan officer explains that the bank must have some **collateral** before it will give you a loan.

> ❖ *Collateral = Something of value that a borrower gives a lender as a guarantee that the loan will be repaid*

For car loans, the bank keeps the **title** to the car *(ownership of the car)* until the loan is repaid. You may drive the car, but the bank actually owns the car during this time. If you fail to repay the loan, the bank will **repossess** the car.

> ❖ *Repossess = To take back a product that the buyer fails to pay for*

The bank also says you must carry fire, theft, and collision insurance on the car while you have the loan. If the car is stolen or damaged, you might decide to stop repaying the loan. The bank does not want that to happen. It wants you to have insurance so that it will be sure to get its money back.

---

4. INSURANCE

Before you go buy your car, you visit an insurance agent. You learn that your state says you must have **liability** insurance as well as the fire, theft, and collision insurance the bank requires.

What is Insurance?

Insurance is a way to protect yourself or your property in case something unexpected happens. When you buy an insurance policy, you pay a certain amount of money called a **premium.** Some insurance premiums are paid yearly. Some are paid some every six months, some every month.

An insurance policy is a contract. This contract tells you exactly what the policy covers.

Insurance to Cover Your Car

Some insurance policies cover the cost of damage to your own property (cars, homes, etc.). Other policies cover damage you may do or the cost of replacing an insured item if it is stolen.

Insurance to Cover Damage You May Do

Liability policies cover the cost of damages to someone else that occur if you are the cause of an accident. In other words, liability policies cover damages that you are **liable** (responsible) for.

An automobile liability policy covers:

- Medical treatment for people injured in a car accident
- Repairs for property damaged in an accident

Liability policies do not cover your own property or your own medical expenses.

Other Kinds of Insurance

In addition to car insurance, you may want to buy a **renter's policy** to cover theft or damage to your belongings in your apartment.

Homeowners' policies cover damage to a home you own and also to the belongings inside the home. Homeowners' liability policies cover medical costs of people injured on the owners' property.

5. GETTING A CREDIT CARD

You are now the proud owner of a car. Your loan is paid off. You have no more monthly payments. The bank has given you the title to your car.

You decide to talk to your bank about getting a credit card.

Another application to fill out! Then the bank will check your **credit history** and your **credit rating.**

> ❖ *Credit history = a record of how well you have repaid previous loans*
>
> ❖ *Credit rating = an estimate of how likely you are to be able to repay new loans*

Because you have a steady job, the bank gave you credit to buy your car. So you have a credit history. Since you paid your car loan on time, you have a very good credit rating.

The bank approves your credit card. With a credit card you may buy things you want now and pay for them later.

Once every month the credit card company sends you a bill showing the total amount you owe the company. This bill lists everything you bought with your card that month. It also lists any unpaid balance you have from previous months and the interest the company charges you for using the card.

The interest rate for most credit card companies is between 1.25% and 1.5% per month on the total amount you borrowed from the company. This is 15-18% per year. This is a very high interest rate. Banks charge a much higher rate of interest for credit cards than for car loans.

Some credit card companies charge no interest if the total amount borrowed during the month is paid within a short time from the time you get your monthly bill (usually 25 days). Other credit card companies begin charging interest as soon as a new charge is posted on your account.

Your monthly bill also shows the minimum (smallest) amount you must pay that month. This is usually 5% of the total you have borrowed. If your credit card purchases total $200.00 in a certain month, your minimum (smallest) monthly payment will be $10.00 plus interest.

Credit cards are very convenient. If you want something now but don't have quite enough money, you can have it now and pay for it later.

Credit cards can also be a dangerous temptation if you don't keep track of how much you can afford to spend. Many people buy too much on credit. Later they find that they can't pay for it all. The products they have bought may be repossessed. The buyer's credit rating is ruined.

6. INFLATION

You've had your job for three years now. You are doing a good job. Your employer is pleased. You have received two pay raises. Things are looking pretty good for you.

Correction. You thought things were looking good until you started to pay your bills this month. Your rent has gone up. You are spending more for groceries. Gasoline is up, and so is the liability insurance for your car.

Your bills are increasing faster than your pay.

What's going on? You are the victim of **inflation.**

> ❖ *Inflation = a rise in the average price level of all goods and services*

Inflation and Buying Power

Suppose that three years ago your monthly expenses (rent, utilities, food, clothing, transportation, health care, entertainment, etc.) totaled $500.00. Now, the same items cost $575.00.

The difference between the old dollar amount and the new dollar amount of your expenses is $75.00. This difference is 15% of the old total. Thus, your cost of living has gone up 15% over the past three years.

> CURRENT COST OF ITEMS = $575.00
> FORMER COST OF ITEMS = $500.00
> DIFFERENCE = $75.00
>
> PERCENT DIFFERENCE:
> $75 ÷ $500 = 0.15 = 15%

The real value of your dollars has gone down. This means that the **buying power** (or **purchasing power**) of your money has also gone down.

> ❖ *Buying power = the amount of goods and services a dollar will buy at any one time*

If your income has gone up at the same rate that prices have gone up, you can still afford the same things you bought three years ago. If your income has not kept pace with inflation, you will have to cut back on your spending.

What Causes Inflation?

The major causes of inflation are:

- Increases in the demand for goods and services
- Increases in the cost of production
- Increases in businesses' desire for profits

Increases in Demand

If the demand for goods and services goes up faster than the supply of these goods and services goes up, then prices will also go up. This results in **demand-pull** inflation.

Demand for goods and services increases when credit is easily available to buyers. Low interest rates for credit or loans encourage consumers to buy more now, planning to pay later.

Changes in consumer tastes can also increase the demand for certain products. If the supply of popular products is less than the demand, an increase in the general price level (inflation) occurs.

For example, in the early 1980s, consumer taste shifted from polyester to cotton and other natural fiber clothing. As the demand for natural fiber clothing increased, prices also increased, resulting in an increase in the general price level of clothing.

Increases in Production Costs

Price increases also occur when the cost of production goes up.

Increases in the cost of raw materials or the cost of labor raise the cost of production. This can lead to **cost-push** inflation.

Increases in Businesses' Desire for Higher Profits

Businesses' desire for higher profits also pushes prices up. This causes **profit-push** inflation.

At any one time, the cause of inflation may be some combination of all the above conditions. One type of inflation may trigger another type.

For example, demand-pull inflation raises the cost of living. This lowers the value and buying power of the dollar. Producers want higher profits to offset the declining value of money. This raises prices even higher. Workers press for higher wages to make ends meet. This raises production costs. Producers must either accept lower profits or raise prices even higher to cover the added production costs and keep profits high.

Once inflation gets started, it is very difficult to stop.

Whom Does Inflation Affect?

Inflation hurts you whether you—

- Spend money
- Save money
- Loan money

The one time it *benefits* you is when you—

- Borrow money

Spenders

If you spend money, you are hurt by inflation.

Inflation decreases the buying power of your dollars. You can avoid some of the effects of inflation by avoiding products whose prices increase the most.

Savers

If you save money, you are hurt by inflation.

Suppose you put $100 in a savings account for a year. The interest rate on the savings account is 5%.

However, the inflation rate is 8%. Your account steadily loses value.

At the end of the year, your money will be worth less than when you opened the account.

If the interest rate on your account had been the same as the rate of inflation (8%), your money would be worth exactly the same amount at the end of the year as when you opened the account.

Lenders

If you loan money, that is, if you are a **creditor**, you are hurt by inflation.

Suppose you loan someone else $100 for a year. If inflation causes the dollar to lose value (and thus lose buying power) during the year, you will be repaid with money that is worth less than the money you loaned.

Borrowers

If you borrow money, that is, if you are a **debtor**, you *benefit* from inflation!

Suppose you borrow $100 for one year. If inflation causes the dollar to lose value (and thus lose buying power) during the year, you will repay the loan with money that is worth less than the money you borrowed.

How Is Inflation Measured?

Inflation is measured by comparing prices from one year to the next. Every month the U.S. Bureau of Labor Statistics (BLS) samples prices of 400 items that most people buy. Together, these items are called a **market basket.** This "market basket" includes food, housing, utilities, clothing, household items, transportation, health care, and entertainment. Price samples are taken in 85 areas across the United States.

In 1950 the 400 items in the market basket cost $24.10. By 1970, the cost was $38.80. In 1990, the same 400 items cost $130.70.

The BLS uses the cost of each month's market basket to figure a **Consumer Price Index (CPI).** To measure inflation, the current CPI is compared with what it was in the past.

> ❖ **Index** = an imaginary number that is used to compare price levels over different periods of time

The increase in the cost of the market basket from one sample to the next is the rate of inflation. If the market basket costs 5 percent more this year than it did last year, the rate of inflation is 5 percent.

Fixed Incomes and Inflation

People with fixed incomes, such as retired people, are especially hard hit by inflation. Their incomes stay the same while prices go up. People in this group often find it hard to survive.

Three years on the job. You are a part of the labor force. You are a consumer. You are a saver. You are a borrower. You have a credit history and a good credit rating. You are a part of the economy.

Think About It

1. If you want to buy a product now, but don't have the money for it, what are your choices?
2. What is meant by *buying on credit?*
3. What is *liability insurance?* Why do many states require car owners to have liability insurance?
4. What is *inflation?*
5. What groups are hurt by inflation? Why is this so?

End of Chapter Quiz

Answer True (T) or False (F):

____ 1. An *alternative cost* is what you give up when you spend money for one thing and not another.

____ 2. Money earned by savings accounts is called *interest.*

____ 3. Getting a *loan* is one way to *buy on credit.*

____ 4. When you get a loan, you must pay back the amount you borrowed plus *interest.*

____ 5. The interest on a loan that a bank charges is usually at a lower rate than the interest the bank pays on a savings account.

____ 6. A *credit history* is a record of your work experience.

____ 7. If you have repaid past loans on time, you are likely to have a good *credit rating.*

____ 8. When *inflation* is high, your *buying power* also goes up.

____ 9. Increases in the demand for goods or in the cost of production can cause *inflation.*

____ 10. If you save money, you are not likely to be hurt by *inflation.*

CHAPTER 18

FINANCIAL INSTITUTIONS

This chapter will look at financial institutions and what they do.

> ❖ **Financial institution** = A business, like a bank or a savings and loan association, that offers financial services to customers

1. THINGS THAT A FINANCIAL INSTITUTION DOES

A financial institution has several functions in our economy. It does all of the following things:

- Provides services to depositors and borrowers
- Makes a profit for itself
- Creates money

Providing Services

A financial institution is a market. It sells two main kinds of financial services to customers:

- Storing money for depositors, and
- Lending money to borrowers

Storing Money

Keeping money in a financial institution is safer than keeping it in your pocket or under your mattress. In addition, money in savings accounts, and even in some checking accounts, earns interest. This interest is income for the depositor.

Lending Money

Financial institutions use part of the money they have on deposit to make loans to individuals and businesses. This is an important service. Most people must borrow money from a financial institution to buy such things as a home or a car. Most businesses must borrow money for equipment or raw materials or inventory that they sell.

A financial institution is not allowed to use all of its depositors' money for loans. By law, it must keep back a certain amount so that it can pay any depositors who want their money. This amount is called a **reserve.**

Making a Profit

A financial institution is also a business. It must earn money to make a profit for its owners and also to pay its operating expenses.

150

A financial institution earns money by—

- Charging interest on loans
- Earning interest from investments
- Charging a fee for storing money

Interest on Loans

Borrowers must pay interest on loans. The interest rate charged for loans is higher than the interest rate paid to depositors. For instance, if depositors earn 6% interest on savings accounts, borrowers would be charged 8% or 9% for loans. The extra interest from loans is income for the financial institution.

Earnings from Investments

A financial institution does not lend all its money to individuals and businesses. It also buys bonds or makes other investments. The interest from these investments is income to the financial institution, just as the interest from loans is.

Fees for Storing Money

Some banks charge their depositors for the service of storing money and for the service of processing checks written on a checking account. This fee is sometimes called a **service charge.** If a customer keeps a lot of money in an account, there may be no service charge.

No matter how it makes money, the financial institution uses its income for operating expenses and to pay its owners a profit.

Creating Money

Financial institutions also create money. You are probably wondering how this can be. Let's look at an example of a bank which keeps a 20 percent cash reserve.

Remember that a certain percent of every deposit must be kept in a cash reserve. But the rest of the deposit can be loaned to a borrower. If the borrower places the money borrowed in another account, the bank's deposits have now grown.

Our imaginary bank has three customers with checking accounts.

- Customer A makes a deposit of $500.00. The bank keeps 20 percent ($100.00) in reserve.
  —The remaining $400.00 is surplus and can be loaned.

- Customer B takes out a $400.00 loan and places the money in an account. Now the bank's deposits have grown to $900.00 ($500.00 + $400.00).
  —The bank must place 20 percent of the new deposit ($80.00) in its cash reserve, but it can loan out the remaining $320.00.

- The next day Customer C comes in. You guessed it. Customer C wants a $320.00 loan. Customer C puts the money into an account.
  —Now the bank's deposits have grown to $1220.00 ($500.00 + 400.00 + 320.00).
  —After the bank puts 20 percent of the new deposit ($64.00) into its cash reserve, it still has $256.00 left to loan.

	DEPOSITS	RESERVES	SURPLUS TO LOAN	BANK'S BALANCE
AFTER CUSTOMER A	$500.00	$100.00	$400.00	$500.00
AFTER CUSTOMER B	$400.00	$80.00	$320.00	$900.00
AFTER CUSTOMER C	$320.00	$64.00	$256.00	$1220.00

Figure 18-1 Bank Loans After a $500 Deposit

The process could continue until the bank had nothing left of the original $500 deposit to loan. By that time, the bank would have loaned a total of $2000—the original loan of $400 to Customer B plus $1600 more.

Look at the Balance column in the Figure 18–1. You will see that as each loan is deposited, the amount of money in checking accounts at the bank (the bank's balance) grows.

Each deposit into a checking account becomes part of the money supply. The money can be used by the depositor to buy things or pay bills.

The example above is about a bank. But the process works the same for any financial institution that accepts deposits and makes loans.

2. DIFFERENT KINDS OF FINANCIAL INSTITUTIONS

There are several different kinds of financial institutions. Three main kinds are:

- Banks
- Savings and loan associations (S & Ls)
- Credit unions

Banks

Banks, also called **commercial banks**, are probably the best-known kind of financial institution. There are two banking systems in the United States today—**state banks** and **national banks**. All banks must have a charter from either a state government or the federal government. Whichever government charters a particular bank also makes rules to regulate that bank.

Both state and federal regulations require that—

- The owners of a bank must invest some of their own money to start the bank. This helps protect the bank's future depositors.
- The bank must keep a certain percentage of its depositors' money **in reserve**—that is, in money form, not in the form of loans. This makes sure that the bank will have enough cash for depositors who want to withdraw their money.
- State and federal regulations also set limits on the size of loans banks can make.

The rules for national banks are more strict than the rules for most state banks. For instance, owners of national banks must make a larger investment in their bank than owners of state banks.

Banks offer both checking and savings accounts to depositors.

- Deposits in checking accounts are **representative money.** They may be used in place of money any time the depositor writes a check.
- Deposits in savings accounts are **near money.** A depositor must go to the bank to withdraw money from a savings account.

Savings and Loan Associations

Savings and loan associations, often called **S&Ls**, are another kind of financial institution.

S&Ls accept savings deposits from customers and make loans to home buyers. Like banks, S&Ls are regulated by the government. S&Ls are required to reserve a certain percentage of their deposits for depositors who want to withdraw their money.

Credit Unions

A **credit union** is something like a private bank. A credit union is set up by a large group of people who are employees of a certain organization (a business, a city, a school district, or a military base, for example) or members of a certain group (a labor union, for example).

A credit union is owned by its depositors, who are called **members.** Only people who are part of the organization or group that set up the credit union may become members of the credit union.

Members of credit unions may open savings accounts or checking accounts or take out loans. Savings deposits in credit unions are called **shares.** Shares represent ownership of the credit union.

Members elect officers and hire employees to operate their credit union. Profits earned by the credit union are paid to its members as interest on their shares.

3. THE FEDERAL RESERVE SYSTEM

The **Federal Reserve System**, commonly called the **Fed**, is the nation's central bank. The Fed is made up of 12 regional banks and 25 branch banks across the nation.

A Board of Governors supervises the Fed. The seven members of this board are appointed by the President and must be approved by the Senate.

The Fed's customers are local banks. That is, the Fed accepts deposits from local banks and makes loans to local banks.

The Fed's depositors are called its **members.** They are also its owners. All national banks must be members of the Fed. State banks may choose to be members of the Fed. About one-third of all state banks are members.

The main jobs of the Fed are to—

- Supervise and regulate banks
- Maintain currency
- Clear checks
- Regulate the nation's money supply

Supervising and Regulating Banks

The Fed supervises banks in order to prevent problems and to keep banks safe. Officers of the Fed, called bank examiners, audit bank records. They also monitor loans and investments made by banks.

Maintaining Currency

U.S. currency (paper money) is issued by the Fed. Bills that are worn out or damaged are destroyed by the Fed and replaced with new bills. The average life of a $1 bill is 13 months.

Clearing Checks

Have you ever wondered how money from your checking account actually gets to the person to whom you write a check? The process is called **check clearing.**

Clearing checks is done by the Fed. It is really a simple process.

Let's suppose that you pay your rent by check. You have an account at the Community National Bank (CNB). You write a check for $250 and give it to your apartment manager.

Your apartment manager deposits your check in the Greystone Apartment account at the First National Bank (FNB).

GREYSTONE APARTMENTS ACCOUNT (AT FNB)	
OLD BALANCE	$1,000.00
DEPOSIT	+ 250.00
NEW BALANCE	$1,250.00

CASH RESERVE AT FNB	
OLD BALANCE	$3,500,000.00
DEPOSIT	+ 250.00
NEW BALANCE	$3,500,250.00

As you see, when your check is deposited, both the account of Greystone Apartments and the cash reserve of FNB increase by $250.00.

Next, FNB sends your check to the regional Fed. Both FNB and CNB are members of the Fed. This means that both have member reserve accounts at the Fed.

At the Fed, $250 is subtracted from CNB's balance and $250 is added to FNB's balance.

CNB's ACCOUNT AT THE FED	
OLD BALANCE	$500,000.00
YOUR CHECK	− 250.00
NEW BALANCE	$ 499,750.00

FNB's ACCOUNT AT THE FED	
OLD BALANCE	$700,000.00
YOUR CHECK	+ 250.00
NEW BALANCE	$700,250.00

Now the Fed sends your check to CNB. CNB subtracts $250 from your account and also from their cash reserve balance.

CNB's CASH RESERVE ACCOUNT	
OLD BALANCE	$2,500,000.00
WITHDRAWAL	− 250.00
NEW BALANCE	$2,499,750.00

YOUR ACCOUNT (AT CNB)	
OLD BALANCE	$1,000.00
WITHDRAWAL	− 250.00
NEW BALANCE	$ 750.00

At the end of the month your bank statement shows that your $250 check has been deducted from your account.

Regulating the Money Supply

The Fed's most important job is regulating the nation's money supply.

If the money supply goes up, then interest rates (the cost of borrowing) go down. If borrowing costs less, more people are likely to borrow money to spend or buy things on credit. Producers are likely to sell more goods. The economy is expected to grow.

If the money supply goes down, then interest rates (the cost of borrowing) go up. People are less likely to borrow money or buy things on credit if interest rates are high. Fewer goods will be sold. The economy is expected to slow down.

The three main ways that the Fed regulates the money supply are:

- Raising or lowering reserve requirements
- Raising or lowering the discount rate
- Buying and selling bonds

Reserve Requirements

As you learned above in the section about how banks create money, banks are not allowed to loan out all the money in their depositor's accounts. They must keep some in reserve.

The Fed decides what percent of a bank's deposits must be kept in reserve. If this **reserve requirement** is low, a large portion of the money on deposit is available for loans. The money supply can grow. If the reserve requirement is high, less money will be available for loans. The money supply will grow more slowly.

For example, if a bank keeps 20 percent of its deposits for reserves, It can loan out $5000 for every $1000 in depos-

its. (The section on how banks create money shows you why.) But if it has to keep 25 percent of its deposits for reserves, it can lend out only $4000 for every $1000 in deposits.

The Discount Rate and the Prime Rate

The **discount rate** is the rate of interest that the Fed charges for loans to its member banks and to the government. The interest rates that financial institutions then charge individuals and businesses are usually higher than the discount rate.

> ❖ **The prime rate** = The best (lowest) interest rate that financial institutions charge their best customers—usually businesses—for a loan. Interest rates for higher-risk loans are greater than the prime rate.

When the discount rate goes up, the prime rate and the rates for all other loans also tend to go up. When the discount rate goes down, the rates for other loans tend to go down.

Buying and Selling Bonds

When a government's income from taxes isn't enough to pay all the government's expenses, the government may borrow money. Governments often borrow money by selling **bonds.**

> ❖ **Bond** = A document that promises to repay borrowed money

The Fed decides when to sell more federal government bonds and when to buy back the bonds.

If the Fed wants to decrease the money supply, it may sell more bonds. The money that individuals and businesses pay for the bonds is taken out of circulation. This leaves less money in the economy. With less money, people are not able to buy as many things. Supply will be greater than demand. Prices drop. This is one way the Fed controls inflation.

If the Fed wants to put more money in circulation in the economy, it buys back government bonds. The money people and businesses get from selling their government bonds goes back into the economy. With more money to spend, demand goes up. Producers are encouraged to produce more goods for people to buy. This is one way the Fed uses to try to make the economy grow faster.

Buying and selling bonds is the Fed's most important way of controlling the money supply.

The Fed and Monetary Policy

The system the Fed uses to control the nation's money supply is called the **monetary policy.**

If the Fed follows an **easy money** policy, the nation's money supply is allowed to grow. The Fed follows an easy money policy when it wants the economy to grow. An easy money policy lowers the cost of borrowing money. When money is easier to borrow, people are encouraged to spend more. The Fed hopes that increased consumer demand will encourage businesses to produce more for people to buy.

If the Fed follows a **tight money** policy, growth of the nation's money supply slows down. The price of credit goes up.

4. KEEPING FINANCIAL INSTITUTIONS SAFE

Why Do Financial Institutions Fail?

Financial institutions are like other businesses. They can lose so much money that they fail. When this happens, the institution's depositors can lose their money, too.

The two main reasons why financial institutions fail are—

- Poor management, and
- Problems in the economy.

Management Problems

A successful financial institution has good management. Good management of a financial institution means that—

- Loans will be made only to borrowers who can repay them.
- The institution will not spend more than it earns.

To get a loan, a borrower must have **collateral.**

> ❖ *Collateral = something used to guarantee repayment of a loan*

If a financial institution makes a loan for a house, the house is collateral. If the borrower fails to repay the loan, the financial institution takes the house. It can then get some or all of its money back by setting the house. The same is true for a car loan. If you borrow money to buy a car and then fail to repay your loan, the lender will repossess your car and try to get its money back by selling the car.

Loans that do not have enough collateral are risky. If a financial institution makes such risky loans, it is likely to lose the money it has loaned. If the institution makes very many risky loans it will go out of business—that is, it will fail.

Some financial institutions also get into trouble by spending more than they earn. Managers may feel that a fancy new building or beautifully decorated lobby and offices will attract customers. But if the institution spends more than it earns, it may fail.

Problems in the Economy

Some financial institutions make a large proportion of their loans to one particular industry, such as agriculture in the Midwest or oil in Texas, Oklahoma, and Louisiana. If an institution makes more than 25 percent of its loans in one industry and that industry declines, the institution may fail even if it is well managed.

Laws to Keep Financial Institutions Safe

Financial institutions in the United States have not always been safe.

During the early days of the United States, those who favored a strong national government and those who favored strong states' rights disagreed about who should charter and regulate the nation's banks.

From 1791 until 1811, all banks were supervised by a national bank, called the **First Bank of the United States.** Banks were required to hold reserves of gold and silver to back up paper money.

But Congress did not renew the First Bank's charter when it expired in 1811.

For the next five years, state banks went unsupervised. People lost confidence in state banks because many of them issued more paper money than they could back up with gold or silver.

The **Second Bank of the United States**, chartered in 1816, tried to bring order back to the banking system. But it was opposed by many who thought that state banks should be allowed to provide as much paper money and credit as people wanted.

By 1837, the paper money issued by many of these state banks was worthless. Many state banks went out of business because they did not have enough gold or silver to redeem their paper money. However, instead of supporting another national bank, states began to regulate their own banks. Most required their banks to keep a reserve of about 25 percent of the paper money they issued.

This system did not bring stability to the nation's banking system, however. By the beginning of the Civil War, 1,600 banks across the country were issuing paper money; most of it had little value.

Congress took steps to create a more stable money supply by passing the **National Banking Acts** of 1863 and 1864. Paper money issued by the states was replaced by a national currency that was good all across the nation. These Acts also gave the federal government power to charter national banks and require all banks to keep gold or silver reserves.

But there was no way to control the money supply of the United States until the **Federal Reserve System (the Fed)** was created in 1913. However, the failure of the Fed to successfully control credit during the 1920s led to the Great Depression of the 1930s.

During the Great Depression, large numbers of people withdrew their savings from banks. The banks' gold reserves were not large enough to cover all of these withdrawals, and more than 5,100 banks failed. Many people lost all their life savings.

In 1933, Congress passed a **Banking Act** and the **Gold Reserve Act** to make banks safer and restore public confidence in the banking system.

The Gold Reserve Act changed U.S. paper money from **representative money** (paper money that represented gold) to **fiat money** (paper money that is valuable because the government says it is).

The Banking Act of 1933 required banks to keep cash reserves on deposit with the **Federal Deposit Insurance Corporation (FDIC)**. Bank deposits were insured up to $2,500.

Keeping Banks Safe Today

Managers of financial institutions have a lot of responsibility. They must make decisions about how to earn profits for their depositors and for the institution's owners. They earn profits by lending money and by making investments. But the money these managers lend and invest does not belong to them. It belongs to the depositors and to the owners of the institution.

The failure of a financial institution is very serious. When a financial institution fails—

- Its owners lose their investment, just as if any other business fails.
- People lose their confidence in financial institutions in general.
- Depositors lose their money unless their deposits are insured.

In order to protect our economy and keep public confidence, financial institutions must follow certain rules made by the government.

Insurance for Deposits

Today, government agencies insure deposits in banks, S&Ls, and credit unions up to $100,000 per account.

- The agency that insures bank deposits is the **Federal Deposit Insurance Corporation (FDIC)**. Most banks are members of the FDIC. Only a few banks that existed before the FDIC was created and who choose not to join are not insured.
- Deposits in S&Ls are insured by the **Federal Savings and Loan Insurance Corporation.**
- Deposits in federal credit unions are insured by the **National Credit Union Administration.** State chartered credit unions are insured by either the **National Credit Unit Share Insurance Fund** or a private cooperative insurance guarantor.

Think About It

1. Describe two kinds of services that financial institutions provide to customers.
2. Who owns *credit unions?*
3. Name two main jobs of the Fed.
4. Why does the Fed require financial institutions to keep some cash in reserve?
5. If you planned to deposit money in a bank, would you prefer one that was federally insured or not insured? Why?

End of Chapter Quiz

Answer True (T) or False (F):

____ 1. *Financial institutions* are businesses that store money for customers and lend money to customers.

____ 2. In order to earn the most profit, most financial institutions loan out all the money that their customers deposit.

____ 3. The fees financial institutions charge customers for storing money and processing checks is called *interest.*

____ 4. Financial institutions use the money they earn to operate the business and pay their owners a profit.

____ 5. By making loans, a financial institution increases the supply of money.

____ 6. Banks that are chartered by the federal government are governed by stricter rules than banks chartered by most state governments.

____ 7. *Credit unions* are financial institutions that are owned by their members.

____ 8. The central bank in the United States is called the *Federal Reserve System.*

____ 9. All checks that are written on U.S. banks are cleared through the Fed.

____ 10. Deposits in banks, S&Ls, and credit unions are all insured by the *Federal Deposit Insurance Corporation (FDIC).*